W9-ARU-071

Ludwig van Beethoven

SIXTH AND SEVENTH SYMPHONIES

in Full Orchestral Score

Dover Publications, Inc., New York

Contents

This Dover edition, first published in 1976, reproduces all the music from the separate volumes of the symphonies edited by Max Unger and published by Ernst Eulenburg, Ltd., London, n.d. In the present volume, the introductions by Wilhelm Altmann (in the Eulenburg volumes these are in their original German with French and English translations) are reproduced in English only—but in a totally new translation, prepared specially for this edition.

International Standard Book Number: 0-486-23379-0
Library of Congress Catalog Card Number: 76-12891

Manufactured in the United States of America
Dover Publications, Inc.
180 Varick Street
New York, N.Y. 10014

Symphony No. 6 in F Major ("Pastoral"), Op. 68

In his *Zweite Beethoveniana*, 1887, pp. 369 ff., Gustav Nottebohm pointed out that sketches for the "Pastoral" Symphony occur on sheets that were originally intended for setting down the score of the Fourth Symphony (completed 1806) and that also contain sketches for the Mass in C Major (completed on September 13, 1807). Nottebohm also prints remarks of Beethoven, of which some refer to the wording of the movement mottoes, while others are general in nature; Nottebohm writes: "These do not tell us much more than what the published headings state, but they do prove that Beethoven thought carefully about the wording." These remarks of Beethoven read:

"It is left to the listener to find out the situations./ Sinfonia caracteristica—or reminiscence of rural life./ All painting carried too far in instrumental music loses its effect./ Sinfonia pastorella. Anyone that has formed any idea of rural life does not need many titles to imagine the composer's intentions./ Even without a description, the whole thing, which is feeling more than tone-painting, will be recognized!" Alongside a sketch for the last movement: "Expression of thanks. Lord, we thank Thee."

Further drafts of all the movements of the "Pastoral" are found in an unfortunately mutilated sketchbook of the first half of 1808, which also includes material for the piano and cello sonata Op. 69 and the two piano trios Op. 70. Nottebohm *(op. cit.*, p. 253) writes: "There first appear sketches for the first movement of the 'Pastoral' Symphony. The beginning of the movement is already in the published form. In general the work on this movement is far advanced, partly close to the published version, partly identical with it. Therefore it must have been begun elsewhere. In the first sketches of the second movement, it is in the first stages of its creation, but as work proceeds, this movement approaches its definitive form and finally attains it. The same is true of all the following movements."

The autograph MS score, presented to the Beethovenhaus in Bonn by Dr. Erich Prieger, contains the following remark intended for the copyist: "NB. Write all the German headings into the 1st Violin part." This part, in the Archive of the Gesellschaft der Musikfreunde in Vienna, has the following title [partially translated], as given by Nottebohm (p. 378): "Sinfonia Pastorella. Pastoral-Sinfonie/ or/ Reminiscence of Rural Life/ (More an Expression of Feeling Than a Painting)." The individual movements are titled [in translation]: "Pleasant, cheerful feelings that awake in man on arriving in the country. Allegro ma non troppo —Scene by the brook.[1] Andante molto moto quasi Allegretto—Merry Assembly of Countryfolk. Allegro—Thunder, storm. Allegro—Shepherd's song. Benevolent feelings, joined with thanks to the Deity, after the storm. Allegretto."

The "Pastoral" was one of the two symphonies that Beethoven offered to the Leipzig publishing house of Breitkopf & Härtel on June 8, 1808, when he remarked: "For several reasons I must attach the stipulation to the two symphonies that they should not be published before six months beginning June 1.—I may very well take a trip toward winter and would thus prefer that they do not yet become known in the summer at least." In regard to the fee, Beethoven, who had first asked 900 gulden for four pieces (the two symphonies, the Mass in C and the piano and cello sonata Op. 69), later became obliging and lowered his request to 700 gulden, promising to add, in four weeks at most, two piano sonatas (the two trios Op. 70) or another symphony, which must have been the Fourth. Beethoven did not reach a final agreement with the firm until September 4, 1808, when he was visited in Vienna by Gottfried Christoph Härtel.

Both symphonies were first performed on December 22, 1808, in the Theater an der Wien. The program refers to the "Pastoral" as the Fifth, and the C minor as the Sixth. Beethoven

---

[1] Nottebohm, p. 375 (cf. also his work *An 1803 Beethoven Sketchbook*, p. 56), points out that the rhythmic motion of this scene is already found in the following passage written down in 1803:

"The bigger the brook, the deeper the tone."

wrote to his Leipzig publishers on January 7, 1809: "You would do me a very great favor, and I sincerely urge you to do this, if you do not publish all the things you have received from me until Easter; I will surely come to see you during Lent; also, do not allow any of the new symphonies to be performed before then, because when I come to Leipzig, it will be a real treat to perform them with the Leipzig musicians, whose uprightness and good will I know so well—also I will correct the music when I arrive."

But nothing came of this trip to Leipzig, since Beethoven did not accept the position of conductor to King Jerome of Westphalia that had been offered him. On March 4 he wrote to Breitkopf & Härtel: "Both symphonies dedicated to the two gentlemen together, that is, His Excellency Count Rasumovsky and His Eminence Prince Lobkowitz—Symphony in C Minor, Op. 60 [published as 67], Symphony in F, Op. 61 [68]. Tomorrow you will receive a list of minor corrections which I made when the symphonies were performed. When I gave them to you, I had not yet heard them—and no one should try to be so godlike that he will not make improvements in his works here and there." On March 28, 1809, he wrote further: "Here you have the piano [the correct reading of this word is probably "small"] corrections for the symphonies. Have them made directly on the plates. The title of the symphony in F is 'Pastoral Symphony or Reminiscence of Rural Life, More an Expression of Feeling Than a Painting.' . . . The best thing would be to send me the proofs with the score that you receive; in a few days you will have everything back again."

The publication of this symphony, in parts, was announced together with that of the Fifth in the news sheet of the *Allgemeine musikalische Zeitung* of April 1809 (p. 50). The title reads: "Sinfonie Pastorale pour 2 Violons, 2 Violes, Violoncelle et Contre-Violon, 2 Flûtes, petite Flûte, 2 Hautbois, 2 Clarinettes, 2 Bassons, 2 Cors, 2 Trompettes, Timbales et 2 Trompes, composée et dediée à son Altesse Sérénissime Monseigneur le Prince regnant de Lobkowitz, Duc de Raudnitz et à son Excellence le Comte de Rasumoffsky par Louis van Beethoven. No. 6 des Sinfonies. Propriété des Editeurs. à Leipsic chez Breitkopf & Härtel, OEuv. 68" (publication number 1337).

The same publishers brought out the first score edition, together with the score of the C minor symphony, at the end of 1825 (publication number 4311).[2]

Beethoven did not add the metronome marks till later, at the same time as those for Symphonies 1 through 5, 7 and 8; all these were published in the supplement to the *Allgemeine musikalische Zeitung*, Leipzig, of December 17, 1817.

WILHELM ALTMANN

---

[2] Cf. the news sheet of the *Allgemeine musikalische Zeitung* of January 1826.

Seventh Symphony in A Major, Op. 92

Because it has been severely cut down, the title on the original MS (in the Music Division of the Prussian State Library in Berlin) reads only: "7. Symphonie/ 1812, 13ten." Probably the thirteenth of May is meant, since on May 8 the composer wrote to the Imperial Councilor and Styrian state attorney Joseph Ritter von Varena in Graz, who had asked him for a new composition for a charity concert: "For the forthcoming concert of the reverend Ursuline sisters, I at once promise you an entirely new symphony." And on July 19: "A new symphony is already completed; since Archduke Rudolph has had it copied, that will cost you nothing." It is important to note that, in an undated letter received by the Leipzig publishing house of Breitkopf & Härtel on June 1, 1812, Beethoven declared: "I am writing three new symphonies, one of which is already completed." The Seventh Symphony, which Beethoven called one of his best in his letter of June 1, 1815, to Peter Salomon, was begun in 1811 at the latest. Drafts of it appear in the so-called Petter sketchbook, which in Thayer's opinion was begun as early as 1809, whereas Nottebohm, probably more correctly, dates the earliest entries to 1811. The main theme of the second movement (Allegretto, A minor) even goes back to 1806. Nottebohm, who in his *Zweite Beethoveniana* (1887, pp. 100 ff.) discusses the sketches for the whole symphony in detail, found this theme among drafts of the second and third movements of the quartet Op. 59, No. 3, for which it was thus originally intended (cf. also p. 86). It cannot be definitely determined whether the theme of the Trio of the Scherzo was really a Lower Austrian pilgrimage song, as Abbot Maximilian Stadler has asserted.

The first public performance of the A major symphony did not take place until December 8, 1813, although the Eighth as well was already completed in October 1812. Probably Beethoven had sold one of his patrons short-term exclusive rights in both symphonies, or else was still hoping to introduce them in a concert of his own; perhaps, since he was thinking of traveling to England, he even wanted to save these symphonies for that purpose. On May 27, 1813, at any rate, he wrote to Varena: "I would gladly have sent you 2 entirely new symphonies of mine, but my present situation unfortunately compels me to think of myself, and I cannot tell whether I may not have to leave here soon as a fugitive; for this you can thank the excellent princes who [by reducing their promised subsidies] have made it impossible for me to work as usual on behalf of good and useful causes."

The A major symphony was played again by December 12, 1813, and then again on February 27, 1814, in one of Beethoven's own concerts.

But publication[1] had to wait until 1816, although by April 29, 1815, Beethoven had sold this symphony and a dozen other works, with rights for all countries except England, to the Viennese publisher S. A. Steiner. The great sensation made by the symphony is seen from the fact that in the March 6, 1816, subscription ad in the *Wiener Zeitung* the publisher announced no fewer than seven versions, including the score; he even brought out an eighth version, an arrangement for two pianos, in December. The title of the original edition reads: "Siebente grosse Sinfonie in A dur von Ludwig van Beethoven. 92tes Werk. Eigenthum der Verleger. Wien im Verlag bei S. A. Steiner & Co." (publication numbers: score, 2560; parts, 2561). The second leaf reads: "Dem hochgebornen Herrn Moritz Reichsgrafen von Fries Sr. K. K. apostol. Majestät wirklichen Kämmerer etc. in Ehrfurcht zugeeignet von Ludwig van Beethoven."

Beethoven did not add the metronome marks till later, at the same time as those for Symphonies 1 through 6 and 8; all these were published in the supplement to the *Allgemeine musikalische Zeitung*, Leipzig, of December 17, 1817.

WILHELM ALTMANN

---

[1] Beethoven was rather dissatisfied with the first edition, since many errors remained in the score and parts. Cf. Max Unger, *Ludwig van Beethoven and His Publishers S. A. Steiner, etc.* 1921, p. 50. Note the German title of the symphony publication. This is the first time that a Beethoven symphony was published in score at the same time as the parts.

Symphony No. 6

I Erwachen heiterer Gefühle bei der Ankunft auf dem Lande

L. van Beethoven Op. 68
1770-1827

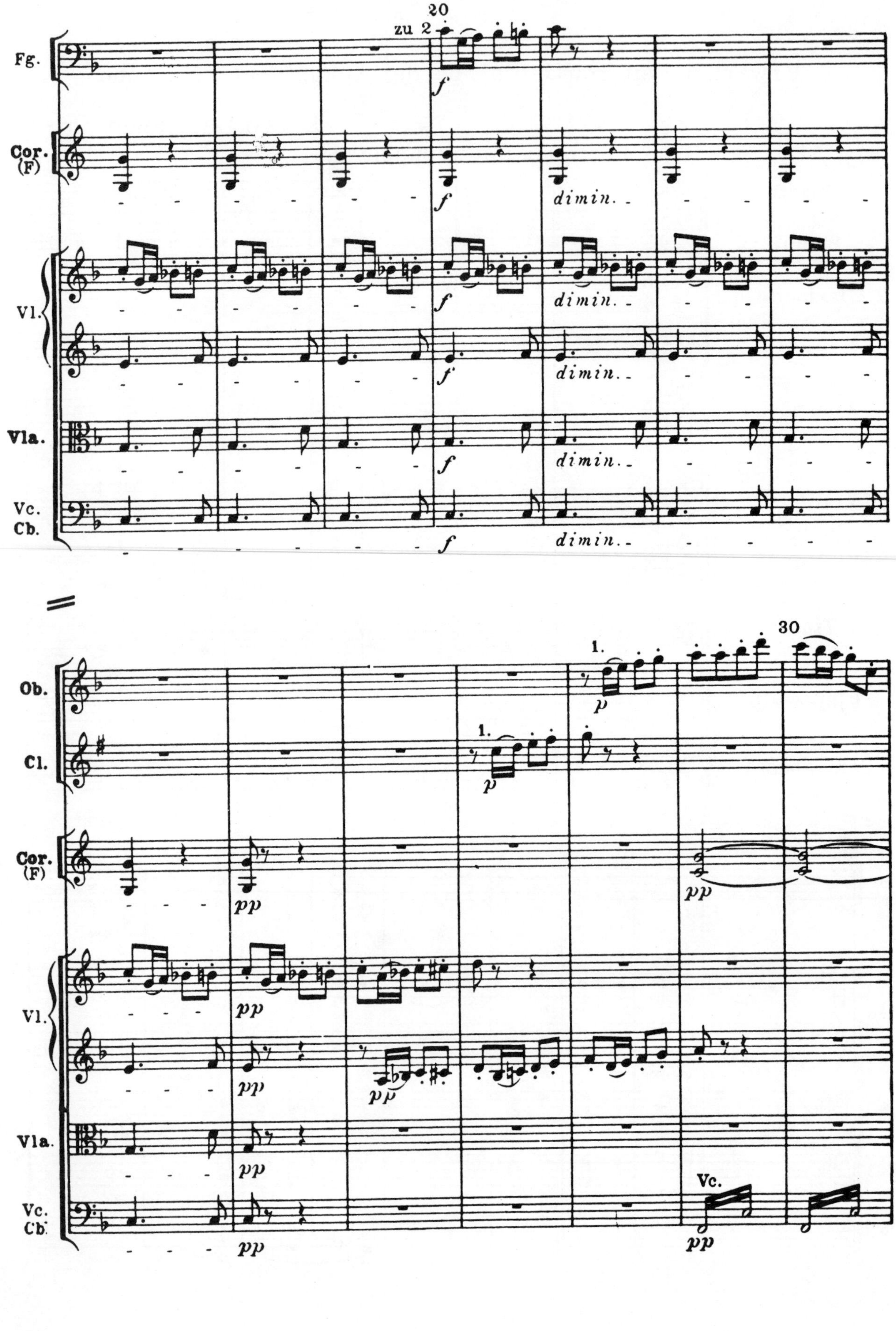

30
Ob.
1.
p
Cl.
1.
p
Cor. (F)
pp
pp
Vl.
pp
pp
pp
Vla.
pp
Vc. Cb.
pp
Vc.
pp

Ob.
Cl.
Fg.
Cor. (F)
Vl.
Vla.
Vc.
p
cresc.
p cresc.
40
Fl.
Ob.
Cl.
Fg.
Cor. (F)
Vl.
Vla.
Vc.
Cb.
f

zu 2
Fl.
Ob.
Cl.
zu 2
Fg.
Cor.
(F)
Vl.
Vla.
Vc.
Cb.
50
fp
fp
p

60
Cl.
Fg.
Cor. (F)
Vl.
Vla.
Vc. Cb.
pizz.
70
arco
Vc.
80
Fl.
cresc.
Cb.

Fl.
Ob.
Cl.
Fg.
Cor. (F)
Vl.
Vla.
Vc. Cb.
cresc.
1.
90
zu 2
f

100

Fl.
Ob.
Cl.
Fg.
Cor. (F)
Vl.
Vla
Vc. Cb.

f f f f f f f f f f
p dolce
p dolce
f f
ff ff ff ff ff
p p p p

110

Fl.
Ob.
Cl.
Fg.
Cor. (F)
Vl.
Vla.
Vc. Cb.

f f f f f f f f f
p p p p p p p p
cresc. cresc. cresc. cresc. cresc. cresc. cresc. cresc.

Fl.
Ob.
Cl.
Fg.
Cor.
(F)
Vl.
Vla.
Vc.
Cb.
120
zu 2
1.
dimin.

130
Fl.
Ob.
Cl.
Fg.
Cor. (F)
Vl.
Vla.
Vc.
Cb.
p
dimin.sempre
pp
f

140
Ob.
Cl.
Fg.
Cor.
(F)
Vl.
Vla.
p
dolce
cresc.
f
150
Fl.
Ob.
Cl.
Fg.
Cor.
(F)
1.Vl.
Vla.
Vc.
Cb.
p cresc. poco a poco
cresc. poco a poco

1.
p cresc. poco a poco
Fl.
Cl.
Fg.
Cor. (F)
Vl.
p cresc. poco a poco
Vla.
Vc.
Cb.
160
1.
cresc. poco a poco
Ob.
Cl.
Fg.
Cor. (F)
Vl.
Vla.
Vc.
Cb.

170
Ob.
cresc.
Cl.
Fg.
Vl.
Vla.
Vc.
Cb.
zu 2
Fl.
cresc.
ff
Ob.
ff
Cl.
ff
Fg.
ff
zu 2
Cor. (F)
cresc.
ff
Vl.
ff
ff
Vla.
ff
Vc.
ff
Cb.
ff

180
Fl.
Ob.
Cl.
Fg.
Cor. (F)
Vl.
Vla.
Vc. Cb.
Fg.
1.
p
Vl.
dimin.
p
dimin.
190
Ob.
Cl.
Fg.
zu 2
p
p
Vl.
p
Vla
p
Vc.
p

200
1.
Fl.
p
Ob.
1.
cresc. poco
Cl.
cresc. poco a poco
Fg.
cresc. poco a poco
Vl.
cresc. poco a poco
cresc. poco
Vla.
cresc. poco a poco
Vc.
cresc. poco a poco
Cb.
p cresc. poco a poco
Ob.
a poco
Cl.
Fg.
Vl.
a poco
Vla.
Vc.
Cb

210
Fl.
cresc.
Ob.
cresc.
Cl.
Fg.
Vl.
Vla.
Vc.
Cb.
220
Fl.
Ob.
cresc.
Cl.
Fg.
Vl.
Vla.
Vc.
Cb.

zu 2
Fl.
Ob.
Cl.
Fg.
Vl.
Vla.
Vc.
Cb.
ff
230
1.
p
dimin.
240

Fl.
Ob.
Cl.
Fg.
Vl.
Vla.
Vc.
Cb.

1. zu 2 dolce dolce pizz.

250

1.Vl.
Vla.
Vc.
Cb.

Fg.
Vl.
Vla.
Vc.
Cb.

260
Fl.
Ob.
Kl.
Fg.
Cor. (F)
Vl.
Vla.
Vc.
Cb.
2.
zu 2
zu 2
zu 2
arco
270
Fl.
Ob.
Cl.
Fg.
Cor. (F)
Vl.
Vla
Vc. Cb.

280
2.
Cor (F)
Vl.
Vla.
Vc.
Cb.
p
pp
tr
290
pp stacc.
pizz.
Cl.
Fg.
1.
pizz.

300

Vl. dimin. dimin.

Vla. dimin.

Vc. Cb.

Cor. (F) p cresc.

Vl. pp p cresc. pp p cresc.

Vla. pp cresc.

Vc. Cb. Vc. arco pp Bassi pp cresc.

310

Fl. ff

Ob. cresc. ff

Cl. 1. cresc. ff

Fg. 1. cresc. ff

Cor (F) ff

Vl. ff ff

Vla. ff

Vc. ff

Cb. ff

zu 2
320
zu 2
Fl.
Ob.
Cl
Fg.
zu 2
Cor.
(F)
Vl.
Vla.
Vc.
Cb.
Fl.
Ob.
Cl.
Fg.
Cor
(F)
Vl.
Vla
Vc.
Cb.
fp
fp
fp
fp
3

330
Cl.
Fg.
Cor.
(F)
pizz.
Vl.
pizz.
Vla.
pizz.
Vc.
Cb.
340
Cl.
Fg.
Cor.
(F)
arco
Vl.
arco
Vla.
Vc.
Cb.
350
Vl.
Vla.
arco
Vc.

360
1.
Ob.
p cresc.
zu 2
Cor. (F)
p cresc.
Vl.
cresc.
cresc.
Vla
cresc.
Vc.
cresc.
arco
Cb.
p cresc.
Fl.
cresc.
Ob.
Cl.
cresc.
1.
zu 2
Fg.
cresc.
Cor. (F)
Vl.
Vla.
Vc.
Cb.

370
Fl.
Ob.
Cl.
Fg.
Cor.
(F)
Vl.
Vla.
Vc.
Cb.
380
Vc.
Cb.
pizz.
arco

Fl.
Ob.
Cl.
Fg.
Cor. (F)
Vl.
Vla.
Vc. Cb.

f p pizz. cresc. arco 390

400
Fl.
Ob.
1.
Cl.
Fg.
Cor.
(F)
Vl.
Vla.
Vc.
Cb.
Ob.
dimin.
p
Cl.
dimin.
p
Cor.
(F)
dimin.
p
Vl.
dimin.
p dimin.
p dimin.
Vla.
p dimin.
Vc.
Cb.
dimin.
p dimin.

410
Vl.
sempre
pp
Vla.
Vc.
p dimin. sempre
Cb
Vl.
p
f
Vla.
Vc.
420
Ob.
pp
Cl.
dolce
Fg.
Cor.
(F)
f
Vl.
pp
f
Vla.
Vc.
Cb.

1.
430
Fl.
p
ten.
Ob.
p
1.
Cl.
p
ten.
ten.
ten.
dolce
Fg.
p
dolce
Cor.
(F)
p
Vl.
p
p
Vla.
p
Vc.
p
Cb.
p
Fl.
1.
p
Ob.
1.
p
Cl.
Fg.
Vl.
Vla.
Vc.
Cb.

440
Fl.
zu 2
Ob.
Cl.
Fg.
3
Cor.
(F)
Vl.
Vla.
Vc.
Cb.
450
Fl.
Ob.
Cl.
Fg.
Cor.
(F)
Vl.
Vla.
Vc.
Cb.

Fl.
Ob.
Cl.
Fg.
Cor. (F)
Vl.
Vla.
Vc. Cb.

460

Fl.
Ob.
Cl.
Fg.
Cor. (F)
Vl.
Vla.
Vc. Cb

470

Fl.
Ob.
Cl.
Fg.
Cor. (F)
Vl.
Vla.
Vc. Cb.

Fl.
Ob.
Cl.
Fg.
Cor. (F)
Vl.
Vla.
Vc. Cb.

480
Ob.
dolce
Cl.
pp
Fg.
1.
Cor. (F)
Vl.
Vla.
Vc. Cb.
490
dim.
pp

Fl.
Vl.
Vc.
Cb.
1.
500
dolce
Fl.
Ob.
Cl.
Fg.
Cor.
(F)
Vl.
Vla.
Vc.
Cb.
1.
p
f
sf
zu 2

II Szene am Bach

Cl.
Cor. (B)
Vl.
Vla
S. Vc.
Vc. Cb.
cresc.
Fl.
Ob.
Cl.
Fg.
Cor. (B)
Vl.
Vla.
S.-Vc.
Vc. Cb.
p
cresc.
fp
tr

Fl.
Ob.
Cl.
Fg.
Cor. (B)
Vl.
Vla.
S.-Vc.
Vc. Cb.
tr
tr

10
Fl.
cresc.
Ob.
cresc.
Cl.
cresc.
Fg.
cresc.
Cor.
(B)
cresc.
tr
Vl.
cresc.
cresc.
Vla.
cresc.
S.-Vc.
cresc.
Vc.
Cb.
cresc.

Fl.
Ob.
Cl.
Fg.
Cor. (B)
Vl.
Vla.
S.-Vc.
Vc. Cb.
fp
cresc.
p
tr
dolce
zu 2
1.
2.

1.
Fl.
cresc.
p
Ob.
p
Cl.
cresc.
p
Fg.
cresc.
p
Cor.
(B)
cresc.
p
Vl.
cresc.
p
cresc.
p
pp
Vla
cresc.
p
pp
S.-Vc.
cresc.
p
pizz.
arco
pp
Vc.
Cb.
20
Cl.
pp
Cor.
(B)
pp
Vl.
pp
pp
Vla.
pp
S.-Vc.
pp

Cor.
(B)
Vl.
Vla
S.-Vc.
pizz.
Vc.
Cb.
Fg.
Vl.
Vla.
S.-Vc.
Vc.
Cb.

Fl.
Ob.
Cl.
Fg.
Vl.
Vla.
S.-Vc.
Vc.
Cb.
Cor.
(B)
zu 2

30
1.
Fl.
cresc.
dolce
Ob.
cresc.
p
Cl.
cresc.
p
Fg.
cresc.
p
Cor
(B)
cresc.
p
Vl.
cresc.
p
pizz.
cresc.
p
pizz.
Vla.
cresc.
p
pizz.
S-Vc.
cresc.
p
Vc.
Cb.
cresc.
p

Fl.
Ob.
cresc.
Cl.
cresc.
Fg.
cresc.
Cor. (B)
Vl.
cresc.
arco
cresc.
Vla.
arco
cresc.
S.-Vc.
arco
cresc.
Vc. Cb.
cresc.
p
1.
dolce
pizz.
pizz.
pizz.
Fl.
Ob.
Cl.
Fg.
1.
Vl.
arco
tr
Vla.
arco
S.-Vc.
arco
Vc. Cb.

Cl.
Fg.
cresc.
Vl.
cresc.
tr
cresc.
Vla.
cresc.
S.-Vc.
cresc.
Vc.
Cb.
cresc.
Fl.
cresc.
f
Ob.
1.
cresc.
f
Cl.
f
Fg.
f
Cor.
(B)
f
Vl.
f
tr
f
Vla.
f
S.-Vc.
f
Vc.
Cb.
f
arco

40
1.
Fl.
p
dim.
pp
Ob.
p
dim.
pp
Cl.
p
dim.
pp
1.
Fg.
p
dim.
Cor.
(B)
tr
Vl.
dim.
p
dim.
pp
dim.
p
dim.
pp
Vla.
dim.
p
dim.
pizz.
S.-Vc.
dim.
p
dim.
pizz.
Vc.
Cb.
dim.
p
dim.

Fl.
cresc.
f
Ob.
cresc.
f
Cl.
cresc.
f
Fg.
cresc.
f
zu 2
Cor.
(B)
f
Vl.
cresc.
f
cresc.
f
Vla.
cresc.
f
arco
S-Vc.
cresc.
f
Vc.
u. Kb
cresc.
f

Fl.
Ob.
zu 2
Cl.
zu 2
Fg.
zu 2
Cor.
(B)
Vl.
Vla.
S.-Vc.
arco
Vc.
Cb.
f
sf
p

Fl.
p
Ob.
p
Cl.
p
cresc.
Fg.
p
Cor. (B)
p
cresc.
Vl.
p
tr
tr
cresc.
pizz.
arco
p
Vla.
p
cresc.
S.-Vc.
pizz.
arco
p
cresc.
Vc. Cb.
pizz.
arco
p
cresc.

1.
50
Fl.
Ob.
Cl.
Fg.
Cor. (B)
Vl.
Vla.
S.-Vc.
Vc. Cb.
cresc.
sf
p

Fl.
Ob.
Cl.
Fg.
Cor. (B)
Vl.
Vla.
S.-Vc.
Vc. Cb.
dim.
pizz.

Fl.
Ob.
Cl.
Fg.
Cor. (B)
Vl.
Vla.
S.-Vc.
Vc. Cb.
pp
dolce
pizz.
1.
Fl.
Cl.
Fg.
Vl.
Vla.
S.-Vc.
Vc. Cb.

Fl.
cresc.
Ob.
cresc.
Cl.
cresc.
Fg.
cresc.
Cor. (B)
cresc.
Vl.
cresc.
Vla.
arco
S.-Vc.
cresc.
Vc. Cb.
cresc.
p
1.
60
Fl.
Ob.
Cor. (B)
Vl.
Vla.
S.-Vc.
Vc. Cb.

Fl.
Ob.
Cl.
Fg.
Cor. (B)
Vl.
Vla.
S.-Vc.
Vc. Cb.
p
p
Fl.
Ob.
Cl.
Fg.
Cor. (B)
cresc.
Vl.
cresc.
cresc.
Vla.
cresc.
S.-Vc.
pizz.
Vc. Cb.
pizz.

Fl.
Ob.
Cor. (B)
Vl.
Vla.
S.-Vc.
Vc. Cb.

p cresc. arco

Fl.
Ob.
Cl.
Fg.
Cor. (B)
Vl.
Vla.
S.-Vc.
Vc. Cb.

zu 2 cresc. f p 1.

70
Cl.
Fg.
zu 2
Cor.
(B)
Vl.
Vla.
S.-Vc.
Vc.
Cb.
Cl.
Fg.
zu 2
Cor.
(B)
zu 2
Vl.
Vla.
S.-Vc.
Vc.
Cb.

Fl.
Ob.
Cl.
Fg.
Cor. (B)
Vl.
Vla.
S.-Vc.
Vc. Cb.
cresc.
1.
pizz.
arco
p
f

80
Fl.
Ob.
Cl.
Fg.
Vl.
Vla.
S.-Vc.
Vc. Cb.
dolce
p
dim.
pizz.
zu 2
pp
arco

cresc.
Ob.
1.
Cl.
Fg.
Cor.
(B)
Vl.
Vla.
S.-Vc.
Vc.
Cb.
Fl.
f
sf
dim.
tr

Fl.
Ob.
Cl.
Fg.
dim.
Cor.
(B)
tr
Vl.
Vla.
S.-Vc.
pizz.
Vc.
Cb.

90
Fl.
cresc.
Ob.
cresc.
Cl.
cresc.
Fg.
cresc.
Cor.
(B)
cresc.
tr
Vl.
cresc.
cresc.
Vla.
cresc.
S.-Vc.
cresc.
Vc.
Cb.
cresc.

Fl.
Ob.
Cl.
Fg.
Cor. (B)
Vl.
Vla.
S.-Vc.
Vc. Cb.

Fl.
Ob.
Cl.
Fg.
zu 2
Cor.
(B)
Vl.
Vla
S.-Vc.
Vc.
Cb.

Fl.
cresc.
fp
cresc.
Ob.
cresc.
fp
cresc.
Cl.
cresc.
fp
cresc.
Fg.
cresc.
fp
cresc.
Cor. (B)
cresc.
fp
cresc.
Vl.
cresc.
fp
cresc.
cresc.
fp
cresc.
Vla.
cresc.
fp
cresc.
S.-Vc.
cresc.
fp
cresc.
Vc. Cb.
cresc.
fp
cresc.

Fl.
cresc.
f
Ob.
p
cresc.
f
Cl.
p
cresc.
f
Fg.
p
cresc.
f
zu 2
Cor
(B)
p
f
Vl.
p
cresc.
f
p
cresc.
f
Vla.
p
cresc.
f
S.-Vc.
p
cresc.
f
arco
Vc.
Cb.
cresc.
f

100
Fl.
Ob.
Cl.
Fg.
zu 2
Cor.
(B)
Vl.
Vla.
S.-Vc.
Vc.
Cb.
pizz.
p

Fl.
cresc.
p dolce
Ob.
cresc.
p dolce
Cl.
cresc.
p
Fg.
cresc.
p
Cor. (B)
cresc.
p
Vl.
cresc.
p
cresc.
pizz.
p
Vla.
cresc.
pizz.
p
S.-Vc.
cresc.
pizz.
p
Vc. Cb.
cresc.
p

Fl.
cresc.
p

Ob.
cresc.
p

Cl.
cresc.
p

Fg.
dolce
cresc.
p

Cor. (B)
cresc.
p

Vl.
cresc.
p
arco
cresc.
pizz.
p

Vla.
arco
pizz.
cresc.
p

S.-Vc.
arco
pizz.
cresc.
p

Vc. Cb.
cresc.
p

Fl.

Ob.

Fg.
1.

Cor. (B)

Vl.
arco
tr
tr
tr
tr

Vla.
arco

S.-Vc.
arco

Vc. Cb.

Ob.
Cl.
Fg.
Vl.
Vla.
S.-Vc.
Vc.
Cb.
1.
cresc.
tr
Fl.
Cor.
(B)
f
110
arco

Fl.
Ob.
Cl.
Fg.
Cor. (B)
Vl.
Vla.
S.-Vc.
Vc. Cb.
p
dim.
pp
1.
tr
pizz.
cresc.
f
arco

Fl.
Ob.
Cl.
Fg.
Cor.
(B)
Vl.
Vla.
S.-Vc.
Vc.
Cb.
arco
sf
p

120
1.
Fl.
Ob.
Cl.
Fg.
Cor (B)
Vl.
Vla.
S.-Vc.
Vc. Cb.
p
tr
cresc.
pizz.
arco

1.
Fl.
cresc. sf
p
Ob.
1.
cresc. sf
p
Cl.
cresc. sf
p
Fg.
cresc. sf
p
Cor
(B)
sf
p
Vl.
sf
p
sf
p
Vla.
sf
p
S.-Vc.
sf
p
Vc.
Cb.
sf
p

Fl.
Ob.
Cl.
Fg.
Cor.
(B)
Vl.
Vla.
S.-Vc.
pizz.
Vc.
Cb.

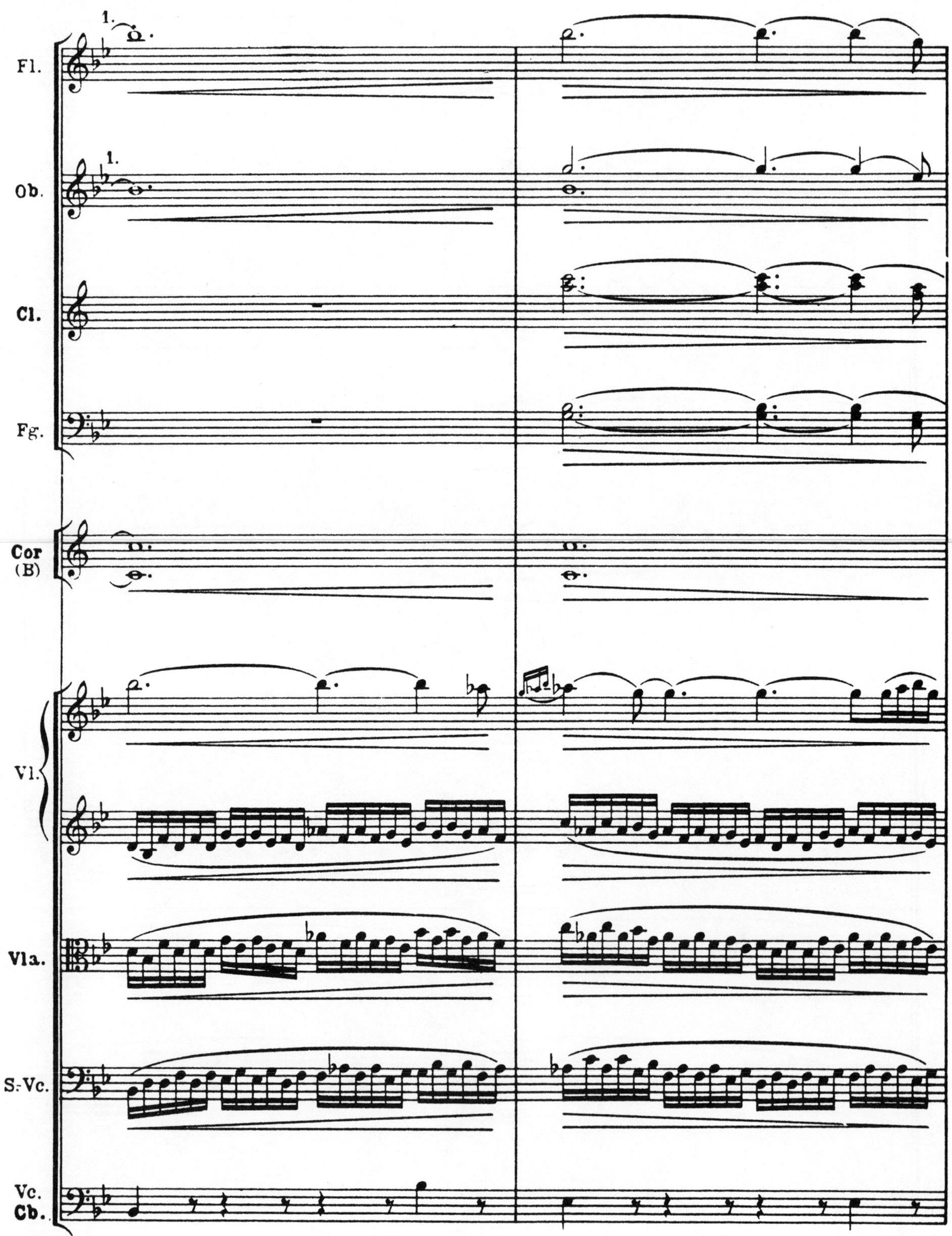
1.
Fl.
1.
Ob.
Cl.
Fg.
Cor
(B)
Vl.
Vla.
S.-Vc.
Vc.
Cb.

Fl.
Ob.
Cl.
Fg.
Cor. (B)
Vl.
Vla.
S.-Vc.
Vc. Cb.
Nachtigall
130
cresc.
tr
Wachtel
1.
zu 2
Kuckuck
p
arco

Fl.
Ob.
Cl.
Fg.
Cor. (B)
Vl.
Vla.
Vc. Cb.
1.
cresc.
zu 2
tr
p
pp
sf
pizz.

III. Lustiges Zusammensein der Landleute

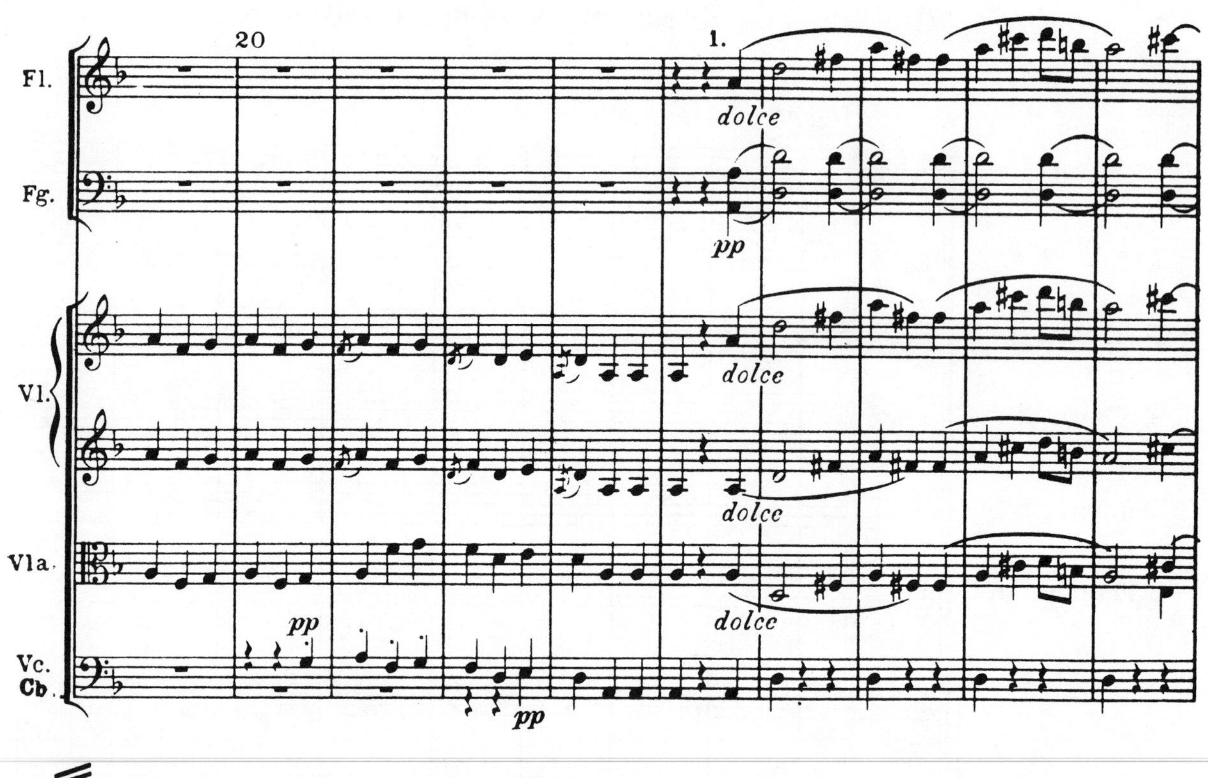

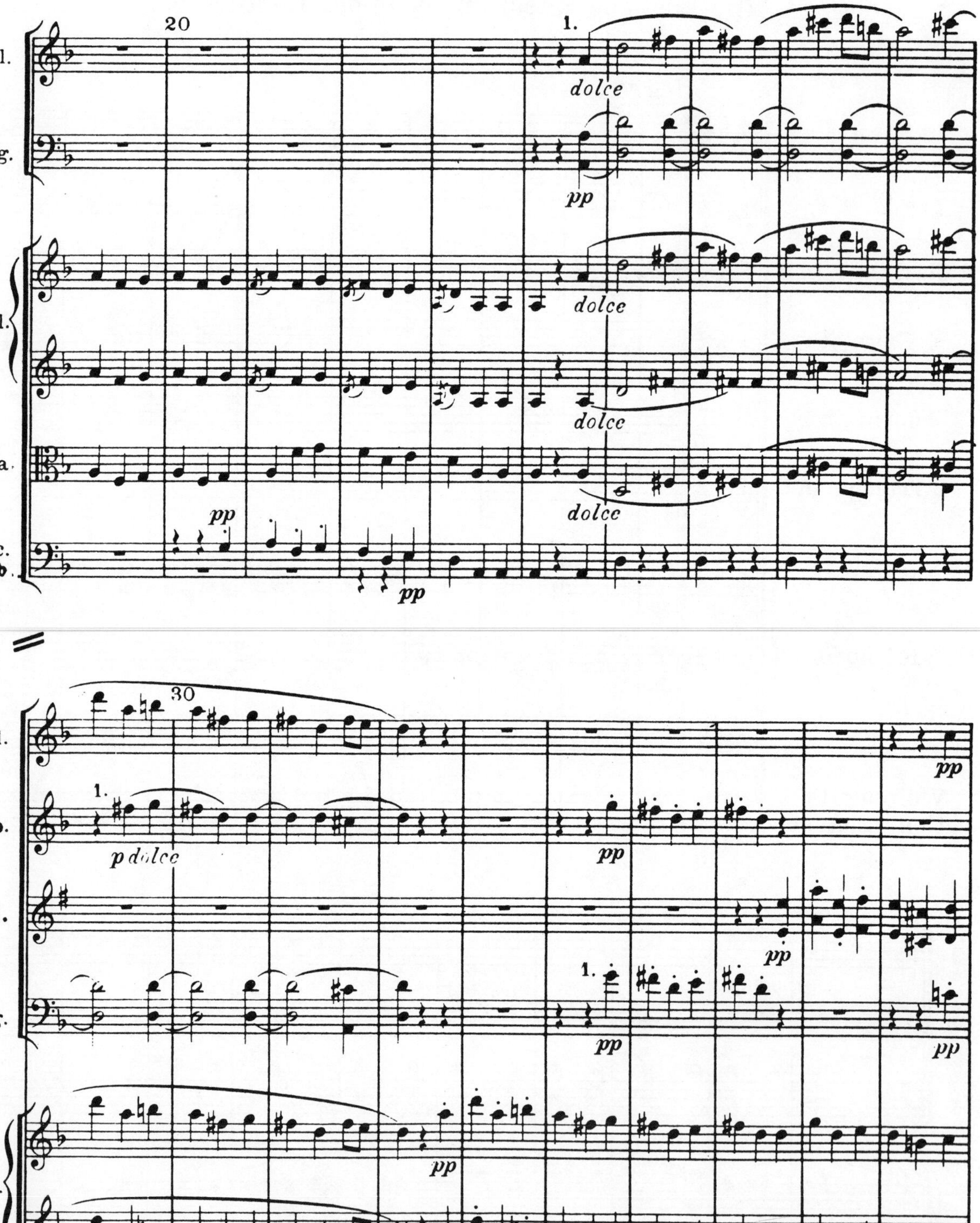

20
1.
Fl.
dolce
Fg.
pp
Vl.
dolce
dolce
Vla.
dolce
pp
Vc.
Cb.
pp
30
Fl.
pp
1.
Ob.
p dolce
pp
Cl.
pp
1.
Fg.
pp
pp
Vl.
pp
pp
Vla.
pp
Vc.
Cb.

40
Fl.
Ob.
Cl.
Fg.
Cor. (F)
Vl.
Vla.
Vc. Cb.
p dolce
p
cresc.
pp
dolce
50
zu 2
ff
sf

zu 2
60
Fl.
Ob.
Cl.
Fg.
Cor.
(F)
Vl.
Vla.
Vc.
Cb.
zu 2
70
Fl.
Ob.
Cl.
Fg.
Cor.
(F)
Vl.
Vla.
Vc.
Cb.

80
Fl.
Ob.
Cl.
Fg.
Cor.
(F)
Vl.
Vla.
Vc.
Cb.
sf
dim.
90
1.
2.
p
cresc.
pp
100
dolce
110

120
Ob.
cresc.
dolce
Cl.
1.
dolce
Fg.
Vl.
130
Ob.
Cl.
Fg.
p
Vl.
Vla.
p
Vc.
Vc.
p
140
Cl.
cresc.
p
Fg.
cresc.
cresc.
p
2.
Cor.
(F)
1.
cresc.
p
dolce
cresc.
Vl.
cresc.
p
cresc.
p
Vla.
cresc.
p
Vc.
cresc.
p

1.
150
Ob.
cresc.
p
Cl.
cresc.
p
Fg.
cresc.
p
Cor.
(F)
dolce
Vl.
cresc.
p
cresc.
p
Vla.
cresc.
p
Kb.
Cb.
p
160
Ob.
cresc.
Cl.
cresc.
p
Fg.
cresc.
Cor.
(F)
p
cresc.
Vl.
cresc.
cresc.
Vla.
cresc.
Vc.
Bassi
Vc.
Cb.
cresc.

sempre più stretto
In tempo d'Allegro (♩ = 132)
Ob.
Cl.
zu 2
Fg.
Cor. (F)
Vl.
Vla.
Vc. Cb.
170
Fl.
Ob.
Cl.
Fg.
Cor. (F)
Vl.
Vla.
Vc. Cb.

180
Fl.
Ob.
Cl.
Fg.
zu 2
Cor.
(F)
Tr.
(C)
Vl.
Vla.
Vc.
Cb.
190
Fl.
Ob.
Cl.
Fg.
Cor.
(F)
Tr.
(C)
Vl.
Vla.
Vc.
Cb.

Fl.
Ob.
Cl.
Fg.
Cor. (F)
Tr. (C)
Vl.
Vla.
Vc. Cb.
200
zu 2
sempre più
f
ff
p

Tempo I
210
Fg.
pp
Vl.
pp
pp
Vla.
pp
Vc.
Cb.
pp
pp
220
1.
Fl.
p dolce
Ob.
cresc.
f
Cl.
cresc.
f
p
p dolce
Fg.
cresc.
f
p
p dolce
Cor.
(F)
cresc.
f
p
dolce
Vl.
cresc.
f
p
pizz.
cresc.
f
p
pizz.
Vla.
cresc.
f
p
pizz.
Vc.
Cb.
cresc.
f
p
pizz.

230
Fl.
Ob.
1.
dolce
Cl.
dolce
cresc.
Fg.
dolce
Cor.
(F)
cresc.
arco
cresc.
Vl.
arco
cresc.
Vla.
arco
cresc.
Vc.
Cb.
arco
cresc.
Presto
zu 2
240
ff
sf
Cor
(F)
Vl.
Vla.
Vc.
Cb.

250

Fl.
Ob.
Cl.
Fg.
Cor (F)
Vl.
Vla.
Vc. Cb.

zu 2

sf

260

Fl.
Ob.
Cl.
Fg.
Cor. (F)
Vl.
Vla.
Vc. Cb.

sf

IV Gewitter, Sturm

Vl.
p
Vla.
p
Vc.
Cb.
p
20
Fl.
cresc.
ff
Ob.
cresc.
ff
Cl.
ff
Fg.
cresc.
ff
Cor.
(F)
ff
zu 2
Tr.
(Es)
ff
tr
Timp.
ff
Vl.
ff
ff
Vla.
ff
Vc.
cresc.
ff
Cb.
cresc.
ff

Fl.
Ob.
Cl.
Fg.
Cor.
(F)
Tr.
(Es)
Timp.
Vl.
Vla.
Vc.
Cb.

Fl.
Ob.
Cl.
Fg.
zu 2
Cor. (F)
Tr. (Es)
Vl.
Vla.
Vc.
Cb.
ff

30
Fl.
Ob.
Cl.
Fg.
Cor.
(F)
Tr.
(Es)
Timp.
tr
Vl.
Vla.
Vc.
Cb.

Fl.
Ob.
Cl.
Fg.
Cor.
(F)
Tr.
(Es)
Timp
Vl.
Vla.
Vc.
Cb.

Fl.
Ob.
Cl.
Fg.
zu 2
Cor.
(F)
Tr.
(Es)
Timp.
Vl.
Vla.
Vc.
Cb.
sf

40
Fl.
a 2
Ob.
Cl.
Fg.
Cor. (F)
Tr. (Es)
Timp.
Vl.
Vla.
Vc. Cb.
2. Vl.
Vla.
Vc. Cb.

50
Fl.
Ob.
Cl.
Fg.
Cor. (F)
Tr. (Es)
Timp.
Vl.
Vla.
Vc. Cb.
sf
fp
f
p cresc.
cresc.

Fl.
Ob.
Cl.
Fg.
Cor. (F)
Tr. (Es)
Timp.
Vl.
Vla.
Vc. Cb.
f
più f
sf

Fl.
Ob.
1.
p
Cl.
1.
Fg.
p
fp
Cor. (F)
Vl.
fp
fp
Vla.
fp
Vc. Cb.
60
Fl.
p
Ob.
Cl.
Fg.
Tr. (Es)
pp
Vl.
Vla.
pp
pp
Vc.
pp
Cb.
pp

Fl.
Ob.
Cl.
Fg.
Cor. (F)
Vc.
Vla.
Vc.
Cb.
pp
p
1.
2.
5
70

Fl.
Ob.
Cl.
Fg.
Vl.
Vla.
Vc.
Cb.
1.
p cresc.
cresc.
1.
cresc.
1.
cresc.
cresc.
cresc.
cresc.
cresc.
cresc.
Fl.
Ob.
Cl.
Fg.
Vl.
Vla.
Vc.
Kb.
cresc.
cresc.
cresc.
cresc.

80
Fl.
Ob.
Cl.
Fg.
zu 2
Cor (F)
Tr. (Es)
Timp.
Vl.
Vla.
Vc. Cb.

Picc.
Fl.
Ob.
Cl.
Fg.
Cor. (F)
Tr. (Es)
Timp.
Vl.
Vla.
Vc. Cb.
sf
ff
f

90
Picc.
Fl.
Ob.
Cl.
Fg.
zu 2
Cor.
(F)
Tr.
(Es)
Vl.
Vla.
Vc
Cb.

Picc.
Fl.
Ob.
Cl.
Fg.
Vl.
Vla.
Vc.
Cb.
p cresc.
sf
fp
cresc.
ff
Vc.
100
f
p

Picc.
Fl.
Ob.
Cl.
Fg.
Cor. (F)
Tr. (Es)
Tbni.
Timp.
Vl.
Vla
Vc.
Cb.
sempre più f
5

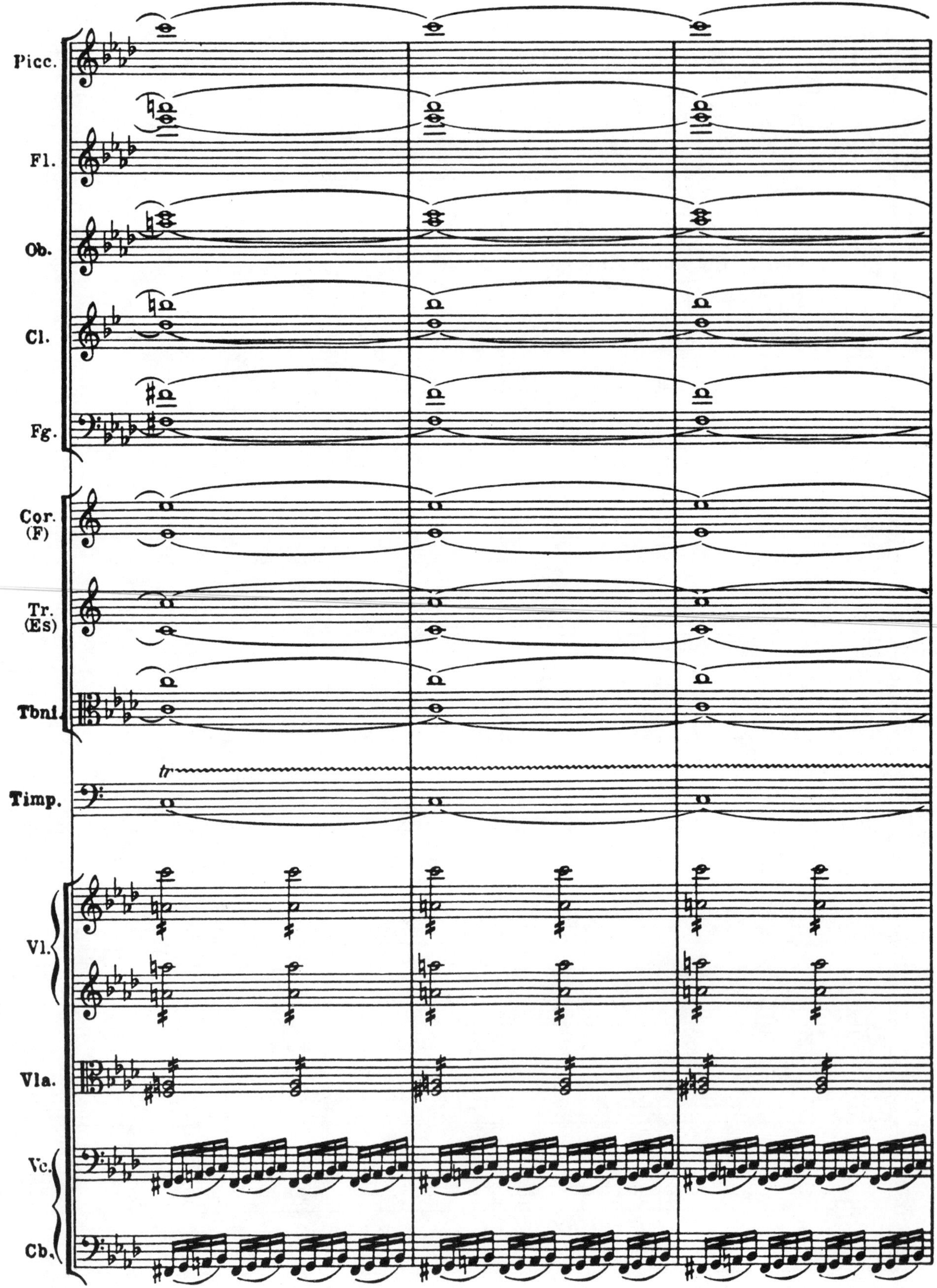
Picc.
Fl.
Ob.
Cl.
Fg.
Cor.
(F)
Tr.
(Es)
Tbni.
Timp.
tr
Vl.
Vla.
Vc.
Cb.

110
Picc.
Fl.
Ob.
Cl.
Fg.
Cor. (F)
Tr. (Es)
Tbni.
Timp.
Vl.
Vla.
Vc.
Cb.
sf
tr

Picc.
Fl.
Ob
Cl.
Fg.
Cor. (F)
Tr. (Es)
Tbni.
Timp.
Vl.
Vla.
Vc. Cb.
sempre dim.
120
Cl.
Fg.
Vl.
Vla
Vc. Cb
sempre dim.

Ob.
sempre dim.
Cl.
1.
Vl.
Vla.
Vc.
Cb.
130
Ob
p
più dim.
pp
Cl.
p
più dim.
pp
Vl.
p
più dim.
pp
p
più dim.
pp
Vla.
p
più dim.
pp
Vc.
p
più dim.
pp
Cb.
p
più dim.
pp

140
Timp.
Vl.
Vla.
Vc.
Cb.
f
p
p dim.
Fg.
dim.
pp

Ob.
Fg.
Vl.
Vla.
Vc.
Cb.
1.
dolce
pp
150
Fl.
Cl.
3

V Hirtengesang

Frohe, dankbare Gefühle nach dem Sturm

Cl.
Fg.
Cor. (F)
Vl.
Vla.
Vc.
Cb.
cresc.
p
pizz.
p cresc.
20

Fl.
cresc.
ff
Ob.
cresc.
ff
zu 2
Cl.
ff
Fg.
ff
Cor. (F)
ff
Tr. (C)
ff
Tbni.
ff
Vl.
3
ff
3
ff
arco
Vla
ff
arco
Vc.
ff
arco
Cb.
ff

80
Fl.
Ob.
Cl.
Fg.
Cor. (F)
Tr. (C)
Tmi.
Vl.
Vla.
Vc.
Cb.

Fl.
Ob.
Cl.
Fg.
Cor. (F)
Tr. (C)
Tbni.
ten.
Vl.
ten.
Vla.
ten.
Vc.
Cb.

Fl.
Ob.
Cl.
Fg.
Cor. (F)
Tr. (C)
Vl.
Vla.
Vc.
Cb
tr

40
Fl.
Ob.
Cl.
Fg.
zu 2
Cor. (F)
Tr. (C)
Tbni.
Vl.
Vla
Vc.
Cb.
f
sf
tr

Fl.
Ob.
Cl.
Fg.
Cor.
(F)
Tr.
(C)
Tbni.
sf
Vl.
Vla.
Vc.
Cb.

50
Fl.
p cresc.
cresc. f
Ob.
f
Cl.
p cresc.
f
Fg.
f
Cor. (F)
f
Tr. (C)
sf
f
Tbni.
Vl.
tr
p cresc.
f
tr
p cresc.
f
Vla.
cresc. f
Vc.
fp
cresc.
f
Cb.
cresc. f

Fl.
Ob.
Cl.
Fg.
Cor. (F)
Tr. (C)
Tbni.
Vl.
Vla.
Vc.
Cb.
p cresc.
f
ff
zu 2
f > p
fp
cresc.
cresc. f

1.
60
Fl.
dolce
Ob.
1.
dolce
p cresc.
Cl.
1.
dolce
cresc.
Fg.
1.
p cresc.
Cor.
(F)
p
p
cresc.
Vl.
dim.
pp
cresc.
dim.
pp
cresc.
Vla.
dim.
pp
cresc.
Vc.
p
cresc.
Fl.
p cresc.
p
Ob.
p
Cl.
p
Fg.
p
Cor.
(F)
p
Vl.
p
tr
p
Vla.
p
pizz.
Vc.
p
Cb.
pizz. p

70
Cl.
Fg.
Cor
(F)
Vl.
Vla.
Vc.
Cb.
cresc.
p
pizz.
Ob.
Cor.
(F)
Vc.
Cb.
arco

80
Fl.
Ob.
Cl.
Fg.
Cor.
(F)
Tr.
(C)
Vl.
Vla.
Vc.
Cb.
ff stacc.
dolce
f
sf
p

Fl.
Ob.
Cl.
Fg.
Cor.
(F)
Vl.
Vla.
Vc.
Cb.
zu 2
90
zu 2
più f

Fl.
Ob.
Cl.
Fg.
Cor. (F)
Vl.
Vla
Vc. Cb.
ff
pp
pizz.
100
Fl.
Ob.
Cl.
Fg.
Cor. (F)
Tr. (C)
Vl.
Vla.
Vc.
Cb.
1.
zu 2
arco
p
f

zu 2
Fl.
zu 2
Ob.
Cl.
zu 2
Fg.
Cor.
(F)
1.
zu 2
Tr.
(C)
Tbni.
Vl.
Vla
Vc.
Cb.

zu 2
Fl.
Ob.
Cl.
Fg.
Cor. (F)
Tr. (C)
Tbni.
Vl.
Vla
Vc.
Cb.
f
ff
sf

110

Fl.
dim.
p dim.

Ob.
dim.

Cl.
dim.
p
dim.

Fg.
dim.
dim.

Cor. (F)
dim.
dim.

Vl.
dim.
p
dim.
dim.
p dim.

Vc. Cb.
dim.
p
dim.

Fl.
pp
cresc.

Ob.
pp
cresc.

Cl.
pp
cresc.

Fg.
pp
cresc.

Cor. (F)
pp
cresc.

Tr. (C)
p cresc.

Vl.
pp
cresc.
pizz.
pp
cresc.

Vla
pp
cresc.

Vc.
pp
cresc.

Cb.
pp
cresc.

120
Fl.
Ob
Cl.
Fg.
Cor
(F)
Tr.
(C)
Vl.
Vla.
Vc.
Cb.
p
p dolce
pizz.
cresc.
arco
pizz.

Cl.
Fg.
Cor
(F)
stacc.
Vl.
pizz.
Vla.
Vc.
Cb.
130

Fl.
Ob.
Cl.
Fg.
Cor. (F)
Tr. (C)
Tbni.
Vl.
Vla.
Vc.
Cb.
cresc.
ff
arco

Fl.
Ob.
Cl.
Fg.
Cor.
(F)
Tr.
(C)
Tbni.
Vl.
Vla.
Vc.
Cb.

140
Fl.
Ob.
Cl.
Fg.
Cor.
(F)
Tr.
(C)
Tbni.
Vl.
Vla.
ten.
Vc.
ten.
Cb.

Fl.
Ob.
Cl.
Fg.
Cor. (F)
Tr. (C)
ten.
Vl.
Vla.
tr
Vc.
Cb.

Fl.
sf
più f
Ob.
Cl.
Fg.
zu 2
Cor. (F)
Vl.
Vla.
Vc.
Cb.

150
Fl.
Ob.
Cl.
Fg.
Cor (F)
Tr. (C)
Tbni.
Vl.
Vla.
Vc.
Cb.

Fl.
Ob.
Cl.
Fg.
Cor
(F)
Tr.
(C)
Tbni.
tr
Vl.
tr
Vla.
Vc.
Cb.

160
Fl.
Ob.
Cl.
Fg.
Cor. (F)
Tr. (C)
Tbni.
Vl.
Vla.
Vc.
Cb.
cresc. f
p cresc.
tr
fp
cresc.

Fl.
Ob.
Cl.
Fg.
Cor.
(F)
Tr.
(C)
Tbni.
Vl.
Vla
Vc.
Cb.
ff
p dim.
crcsc.
Cl
Fg.
Vl.
Vla.
Vc.
pp

170

Fl.
Ob.
1.
p cresc.
Cl.
cresc.
Fg.
cresc.
Cor. (F)
p cresc.
Vl.
cresc.
cresc.
Vla
cresc.

Fl.
f
ff
Ob.
f
ff
Cl.
f
ff
Fg.
f
zu 2
ff
p
Cor. (F)
f
ff
Tr. (C)
f
Vl.
f 3
3
ff
f 3
3
ff
Vla.
f
ff
Vc.
f
ff
p
Cb.
f
ff

180
Fl.
Ob.
Fg.
2.Vl.
Vc.
Cb.
1.
p cresc.
1.
p cresc.
cresc.
p cresc.
cresc.
pizz.
p
cresc.
arco
190
Fl.
Ob.
Cl.
Fg.
Cor. (F)
Tr. (C)
Tbni.
Vl.
Vla.
Vc.
Cb.
cresc.
ff
p cresc.
p cresc.

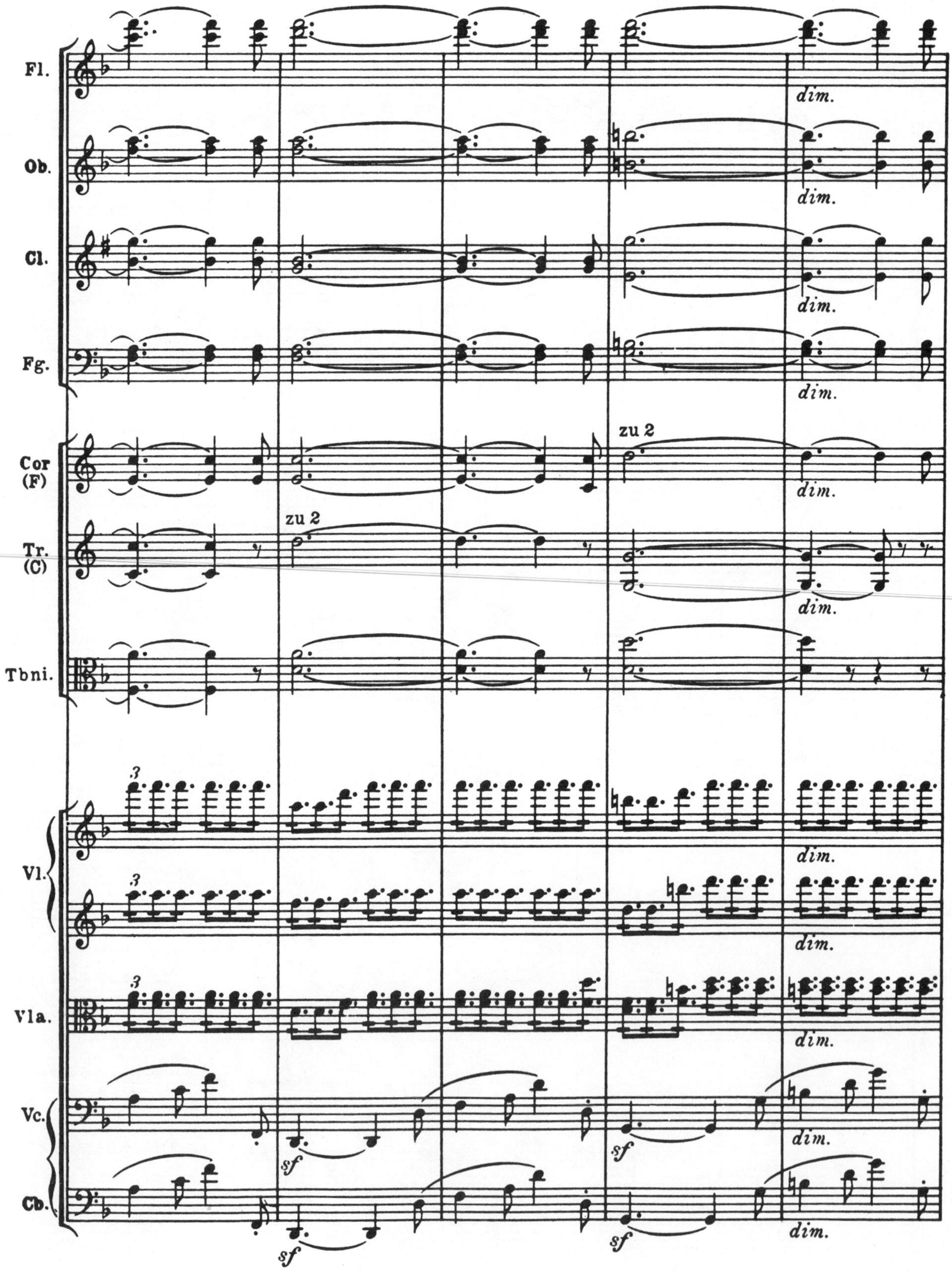
Fl.
Ob.
Cl.
Fg.
Cor
(F)
Tr.
(C)
Tbni.
Vl.
Vla.
Vc.
Cb.
zu 2
zu 2
dim.
sf
3

Ob.
Cl.
Fg.
Vl.
Vla
Vc.
1.
p cresc.
pp
cresc.
200
Fl.
Ob.
Cl.
Fg.
Cor (F)
Tr. (C)
Vl.
Vla.
Vc.
Cb.
p cresc.
f

Fl.
Ob.
Cl.
Fg.
zu 2
ff
p
Cor. (F)
Tr. (C)
Vl.
Vla.
Vc.
Cb.
210
1.
p cresc.
2.Vl.
cresc.
pizz.

Fl.
cresc.
Ob.
1.
p
cresc.
Fg.
p cresc.
Cor
(F)
cresc.
2. Vl.
cresc.
Vla.
Vc.
Cb.
Fl.
cresc.
Ob.
cresc.
Cl.
1.
cresc.
cresc.
Fg.
1.
cresc.
Cor.
(F)
cresc.
Vl.
cresc.
Vla.
Vc.
arco
Cb.

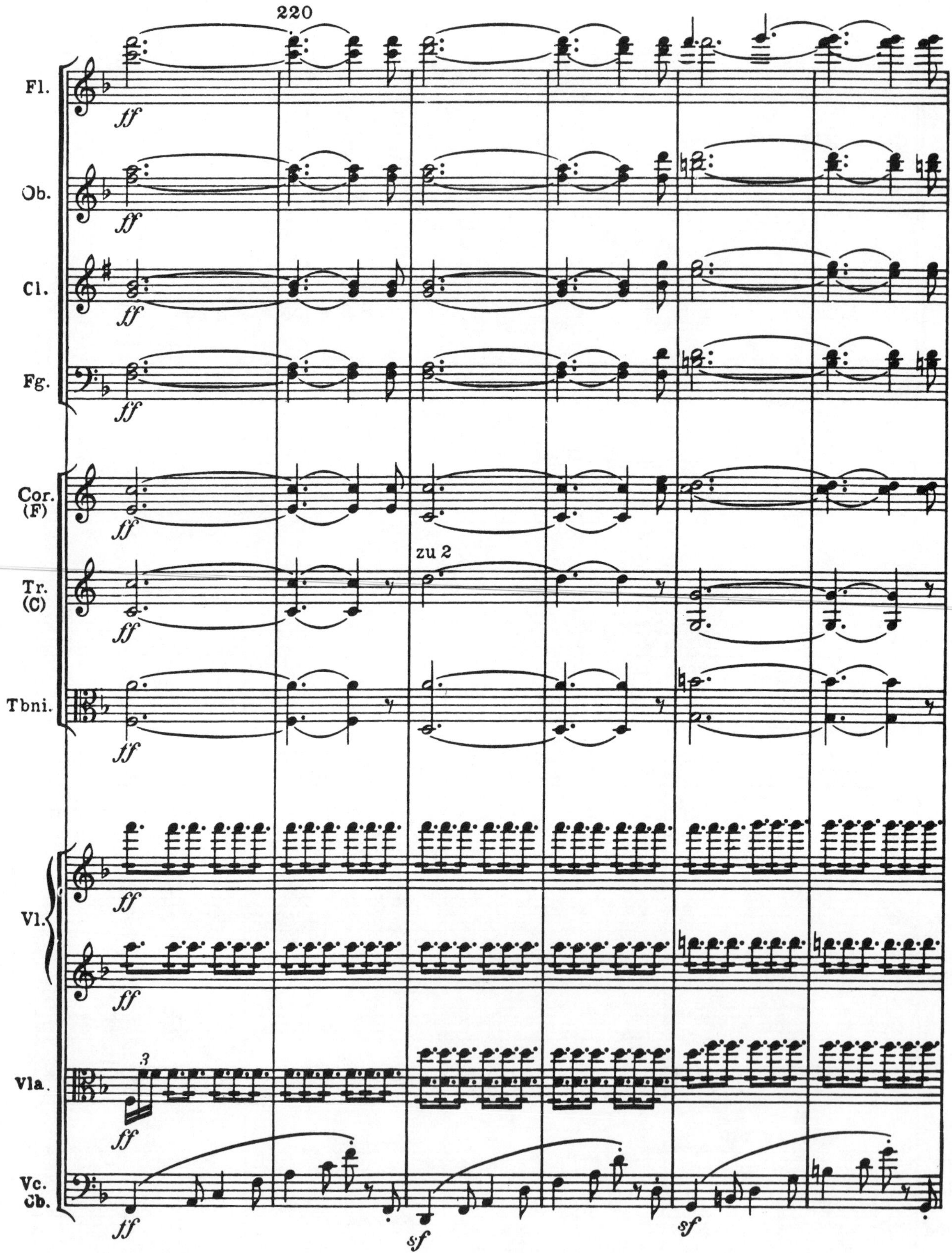
220
Fl.
Ob.
Cl.
Fg.
Cor. (F)
Tr. (C)
zu 2
Tbni.
Vl.
Vla.
Vc. Cb.
ff
sf
3

Fl.
Ob.
Cl.
Fg.
Cor. (F)
Tr. (C)
Tbni.
Vl.
Vla
Vc. Cb.
1
230
zu 2
sf
sf

Fl.
Ob.
Cl.
Fg.
Cor.
(F)
Vl.
Vla.
Vc.
Cb.
dim.
1.
p
più p
240
pp
pp sotto voce
cresc.

250

Fl. *f*

Ob. *f* *p dolce* *p*

Cl. *f* *p*

zu 2

Fg. *f* *p dolce*

Cor. (F) *f* *p dolce* *p*

Vl. *f* *sotto voce*

f *sotto voce*

Vla. *f* *sotto voce*

Vc. Cb. *sotto voce*

Fl. *cresc.* *f* *dim.* 1. *p*

Ob. *cresc.* *f* *dim.* *p*

Cl. *cresc.* *f* *dim.* *p*

Fg. *cresc.* *f* *dim.* *p*

Cor (F) *cresc.* *f* *dim.* *p*

Tr. (C) *f* *dim.*

Tbni. *f*

Vl. *cresc.* *f* *dim.* *p*

cresc. *f* *dim.* *p*

Vla. *cresc.* *dim.* *p*

stacc.

Vc. Cb. *cresc.* *f* *dim.* *p*

260
Fl.
pp
ff
1.
Ob.
pp
ff
1.
Cl.
pp
ff
Fg.
ff
1. con Sord.
Cor.
(F)
pp
ff
Tr.
(C)
ff
Tbni.
ff
Vl.
pp
ff
pp
pp
ff
Vla.
pp
pp
ff
Vc.
Cb.
pp
pp
ff

Symphony No. 7

I

Ludwig van Beethoven, Op. 92
1770-1827

1.
10
Fl.
Ob.
Cl.
Fg.
Cor. (A)
Vl.
Vla.
Vc. Cb.
dimin.
pp
dolce
Tr. (D)
Timp.
cresc.
p cresc.
ff
sf

Fl.
Ob.
Cl.
Fg.
zu 2
Cor. (A)
Tr. (D)
zu 2
Timp.
Vl.
ff
sf
sf
sf
sf
sf
Vla.
Vc. Cb.

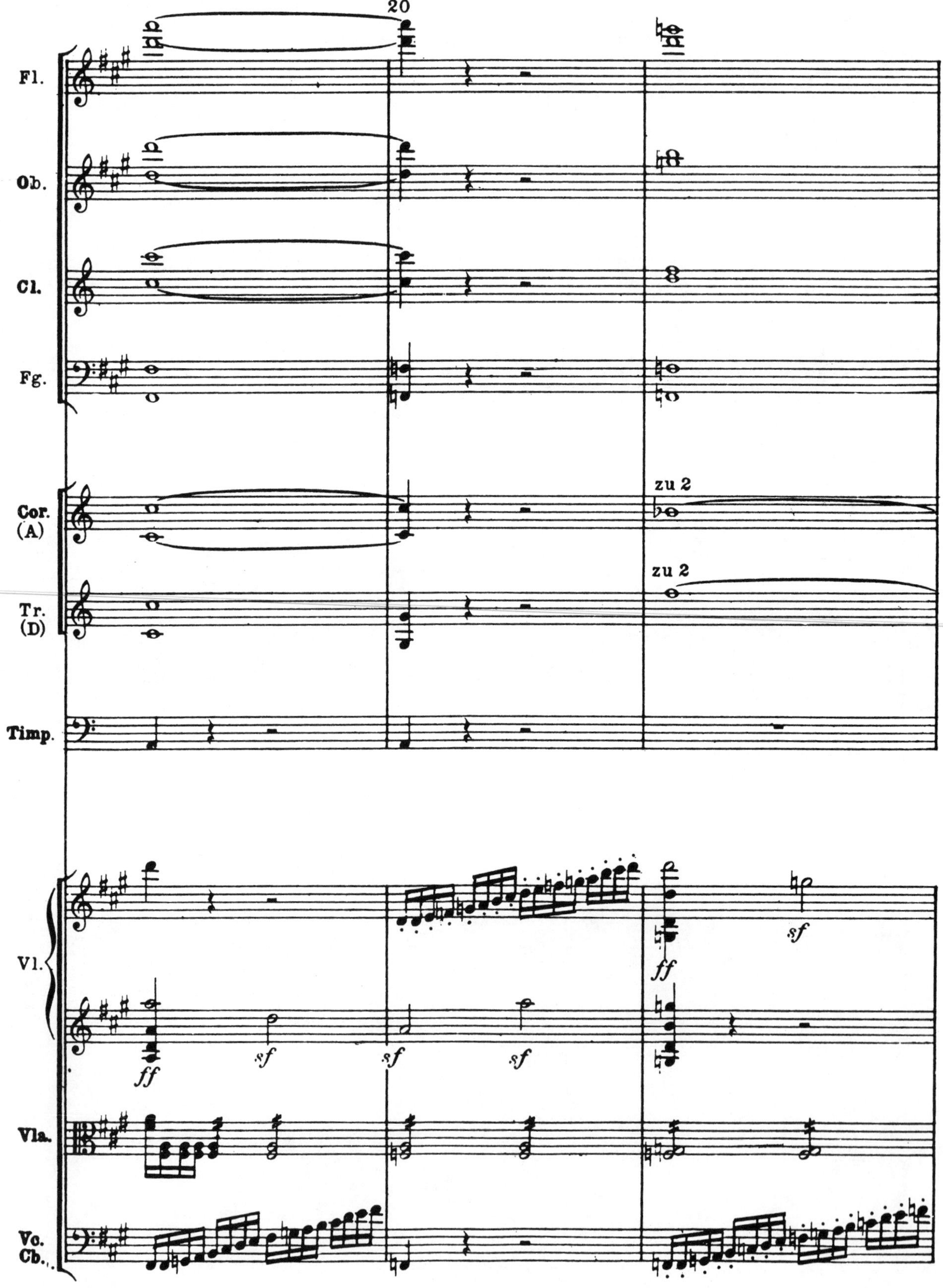
20
Fl.
Ob.
Cl.
Fg.
Cor. (A)
Tr. (D)
zu 2
zu 2
Timp.
Vl.
ff
sf
sf
sf
ff
sf
Vla.
Vc. Cb.

Fl.
dimin.
Ob.
dimin.
p dolce
Cl.
p dolce
Fg.
dimin.
p dolce
Cor.
(A)
p
Tr.
(D)
p
Timp
p
Vl.
dimin.
p
p
dimin.
p
p
Vla.
dimin.
p
Vc.
Cb.
dimin.
p
Ob.
pp
Cl.
Fg.
pp
Vl.
tr
tr
tr
tr
pp
pp
Vla.
Vc.
Cb.
pp
pp

80
Fl.
Ob.
Fg.
Vl.
Vla
Vc.
Cb.
pp
cresc.
Cl.
Cor. (A)
Tr. (D)
Timp.
Vc. Cb.
zu 2
ff
sf
Bassi

Fl.
Ob.
Cl.
Fg.
Cor. (A)
Tr. (D)
Timp.
Vl.
Vla.
Vc. Cb.
sf
ff

40
Fl.
Ob.
Cl.
Fg.
Cor. (A)
Tr. (D)
Timp.
Vl.
Vla.
Vc. Cb.
sf
ff
dimin.
p
p dolce
pizz.
tr
1.

Fl.
Ob.
Cl.
Fg.
Vl.
Vla.
Vc.
Cb.
pp
cresc.
tr
arco
50
Cor.
(A)

Fl.
Ob.
Cl.
Fg.
Cor. (A)
Tr. (D)
Timp.
Vl.
Vla.
Vc. Cb.
zu2
1.
ff
fp
ffp
p
60

Vivace (♩. = 104)
Fl.
Ob.
Cl.
Fg.
Cor. (A)
Vl.
Vla.
Vc. Cb.
sempre p
cresc.
p
70

80
zu 2
p
Fl.
Ob.
Cl.
Fg.
Cor. (A)
Vl.
Vla.
Vc. Cb.
sfp
f
sf
zu 2

90
Fl.
Hb.
Cl.
Fg.
Cor. (A)
Tr. (D)
Timp.
Vl.
Br.
Vc. u.Kb.
sf
ff
sempre ff
f

Fl.
Ob.
Cl.
Fg.
Cor. (A)
Tr. (D)
Timp.
Vl.
Vla.
Vc. Cb.

Fl.
Ob.
Cl.
zu 2
Fg.
zu 2
Cor.
(A)
Tr.
(D)
Timp.
Vl.
Vla.
Vc.
Cb.

100
Fl.
Ob.
Cl.
Fg.
Cor. (A)
Tr. (D)
Timp.
Vl.
Vla.
Vc. Cb.
1.
p cresc.
p
cresc.

Fl.
Ob.
Cl.
Fg.
Cor.
(A)
Tr.
(D)
Timp.
Vl.
Vla.
Vc.
Cb.
stacc.

110
Fl.
Ob.
Cl.
Fg.
Cor. (A)
Tr. (D)
Timp.
Vl.
Vla.
Vc. Cb.
Fl.
Ob.
Cl.
Fg.
Vl.
Vla.
Vc. Cb.

120
Fl.
Ob.
Cl.
Fg.
Cor. (A)
Vl.
Vla.
Vc. Cb.
cresc.
f
p
Tr. (D)
zu 2
sf

130

Fl. Hb. Kl. Fg. Cor. (A) Vl. Vla Vc. Cb

p *dolce* zu 2 *sf* *p* *dolce*

Fl. Hb. Kl. Fg. Cor. (A) Tr. (D) Timp. Vl. Vla. Vc. Cb.

zu 2 *f* zu 2 *f*

Ob.
Fg.
Vl.
Vla.
Vc.
Cb.
1.
140
p
pp
dimin.
Cl.
cresc.
p cresc.
cresc. poco a poco

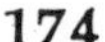
150
Fl.
Ob.
Fg.
Vl.
Vla.
Vc.
Cb.
1.
p cresc.
cresc.
Cl.
Cor.
(A)
Tr.
(D)
zu 2
Timp.
ff
pp

160
Fl.
cresc.
ff
Ob.
cresc.
ff
Cl.
ff
Fg.
cresc.
ff
Hrn.
(A)
ff
zu 2
Tr.
(D)
ff
Timp.
ff
Vl.
cresc.
ff
cresc.
ff
Vla.
cresc.
ff
Vc.
cresc.
ff
Cb.
ff

1.
Fl.
pp
cresc.
ff
sf
zu 2
Ob.
Cl.
Fg.
Cor. (A)
Tr. (D)
Timp.
Vl.
Vla.
Vc. Cb.
Bassi

zu 2
zu 2
170
Fl.
Ob.
zu 2
zu 2
Cl.
zu 2
zu 2
Fg.
Cor. (A)
Tr. (D)
Timp.
ten.
ten.
Vl.
Vla.
ten.
Vc. Cb.
sf

zu 2
Fl.
zu 2
Ob.
Cl.
Fg.
Cor.
(A)
Tr.
(D)
Timp.
Vl.
Vla.
Vc.
Cb.
ff
180
Fl.
Ob.
Cl.
Fg.
zu 2
Cor.
(A)
Vl.
Vla.
Vc.
Cb.
ff
pp

Fg.
1.
pp
Vl.
Vla
pp
Vc.
Cb.
pp
190
Fl.
1.
pp
cresc.
Ob.
1.
pp
cresc.
Fg.
1.
pp
cresc.
Vl.
cresc.
cresc.
Vla.
cresc.
Vc.
Cb.
cresc.

200
Fl.
Ob
Fg.
Vl.
Vla.
Vc.
Cb.
Fl.
Ob.
Cl.
Fg.
zu 2
Cor.
(A)
zu 2
Tr.
(D)
Timp.
Vl.
Via
Vc.
Cb.

Fl.
ff
Ob.
ff
Cl.
ff
Fg.
ff
Cor. (A)
ff
Tr. (D)
ff
Timp.
Vl.
ff
ff
Vla.
ff
Vc. Cb.
ff

210
Fl.
Ob.
Cl.
Fg.
Cor. (A)
Tr. (D)
zu 2
Timp.
Vl.
Vla.
Vc. Cb.

Fl.
Ob.
Cl.
Fg.
Cor. (A)
Tr. (D)
Timp.
Vl.
Vla.
Vc. Cb.
zu 2
sf
ff
220
1.
p
pp
Kb.
Vc.
Bassi

Fl.
Ob.
Cl
Fg.
Vl.
Vla.
Vc.
Cb.
1.
p
230
Cor.
(A)

Ob.
cresc. poco a poco
Cl.
cresc. poco a poco
Fg.
cresc. poco a poco
Cor. (A)
cresc. poco a poco
Vl.
cresc. poco a poco
cresc. poco a poco
Vla.
cresc. poco a poco
Vc. Cb.
cresc. poco a poco

240
zu 2
Fl.
cresc.
Ob.
Cl.
Fg.
Cor. (A)
Vl.
Vla.
Vc. Cb.

Fl.
Ob.
Cl.
Fg.
Vl.
Vla.
Vc.
Cb.
250
f
zu 2
Cor.
(A)
Tr.
(D)
Timp.
ff

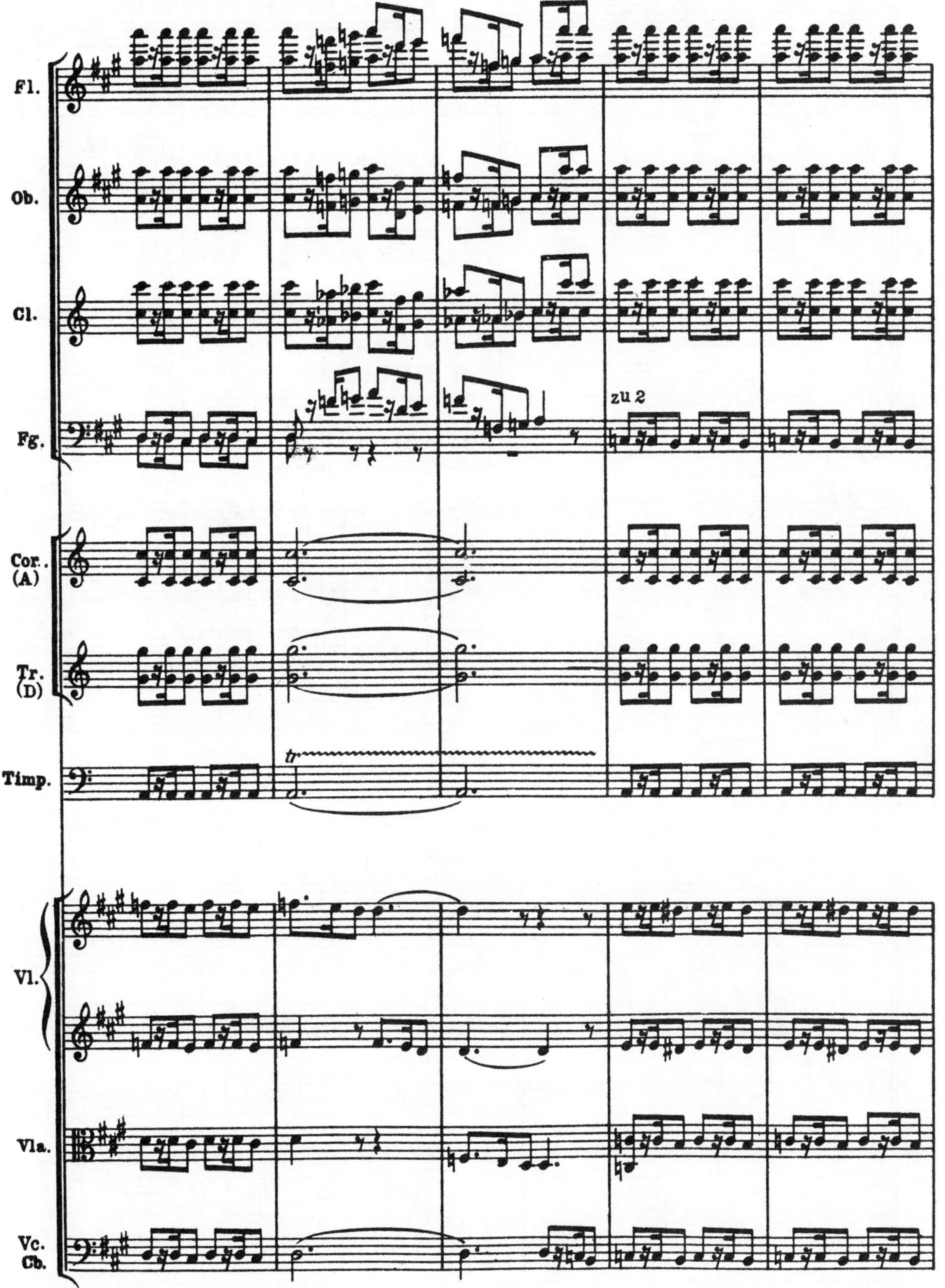
Fl.
Ob.
Cl.
Fg.
zu 2
Cor.
(A)
Tr.
(D)
Timp.
tr
Vl.
Vla.
Vc.
Cb.

260
zu 2
Fl.
Ob.
Cl.
Fg.
Cor.
(A)
Tr.
(D)
Timp.
Vl.
Vla.
Vc.
Cb.

270
Fl.
Cl.
Cor. (A)
Vl.
Vla.
Vc. Cb.
1.
1.
più f
più f
più f
Fl.
Ob.
Cl.
Fg.
Cor. (A)
Tr. (D)
Timp.
Vl.
Vla.
Vc. Cb.
più f
più f
f
più f
f
più f
ff
3

280
Fl.
Ob.
Cl.
Fg.
Cor. (A)
Tr. (D)
Timp.
Vl.
Vla.
Vc. Cb.

Fl.
Ob.
Cl.
Fg.
Cor. (A)
Tr. (D)
Timp
Vl.
Vla.
Vc. Cb.

Fl.
Ob.
Cl.
Fg.
Cor. (A)
Tr. (D)
Timp.
Vl.
Vla
Vc. Cb.
zu 2
290
zu 2
zu 2
sf
sf
sf
sf

Fl.
sf
Ob.
sf
Cl.
sf
Fg.
sf
Cor. (A)
zu 2
Tr. (D)
Timp.
Vl.
Vla
Vc. Cb.

Fl.
Ob.
Cl.
Fg.
Cor.
(A)
Tr.
(D)
Timp
Vl.
Vla.
Vc.
Cb.
p
p
p
p
p

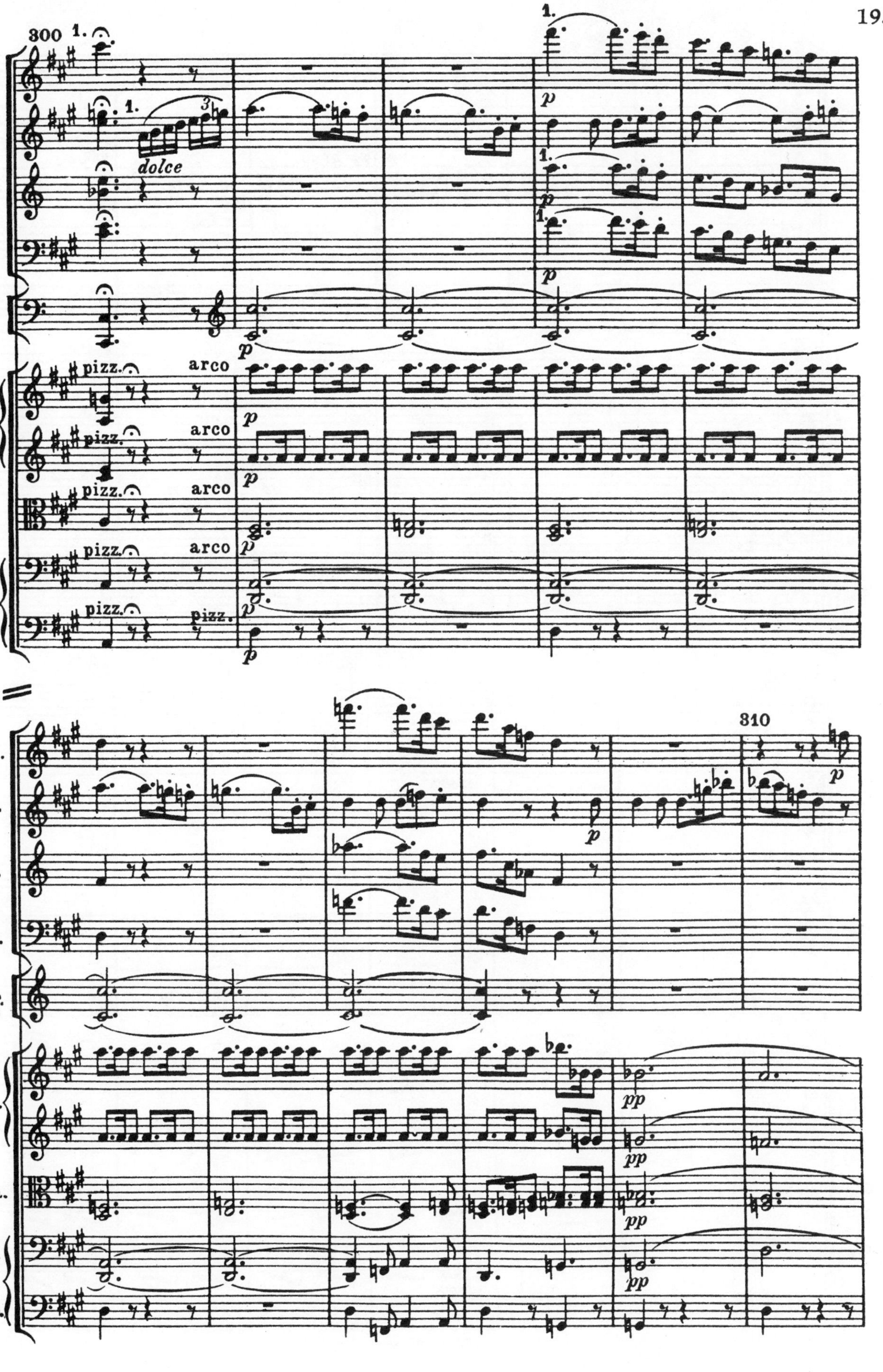
300
1.
Fl.
Ob.
dolce
Cl.
Fg.
Cor. (A)
pizz.
arco
Vl.
Vla.
Vc.
Cb.
p
pp
310

Fl.
Ob.
Cl.
Fg.
Timp.
pp sempre
Vl.
pp sempre
pp sempre
Vla.
pp sempre
Vc.
pp sempre
Cb.
320
Fl.
cresc.
Ob.
cresc.
Cl.
cresc.
Fg.
cresc.
Cor.
(A)
cresc.
Timp.
cresc.
Vl.
cresc.
cresc.
Vla.
cresc.
Vc.
cresc.
Cb.
cresc.

Fl.
Ob.
Cl.
Fg.
Cor. (A)
Tr. (D)
Timp.
Vl.
Vla.
Vc. Cb.
Bassi
330
1.
cresc.

1.
Fl.
Ob.
Cl.
Fg.
Cor.
(A)
Tr.
(D)
zu 2
Timp.
Vl.
Vla.
Vc.
Cb.

Fl.
Ob.
Cl.
Fg.
Cor. (A)
Tr. (D)
Timp.
Vl.
Vla.
Vc. Cb.

f
zu 2

340

Fl.
Cl.
Fg.
Cor. (A)
Vl.
Vla.
Vc. Cb.

p
dolce
sf
p dolce

350

1.

Fl.
ff
p

Ob.
ff

Cl.
ff

Fg.
ff
1
p

Cor. (A)
ff

Tr. (D)
ff

Timp.
ff

Vl.
ff
dim.
ff
dim.

Vla.
ff
dim.

Vc. Cb.
ff
Kb.
Vc.
dim.

Fl.
pp
pp

Fg
pp

Vl.
p
pp
pp
p
pp
pp

Vla.
p
pp
pp

Vc. Cb.
p
pp
pp

860
Fl.
Ob.
Cl.
Fg.
Vl.
Vla.
Vc.
Cb.
cresc.
1.
p cresc.
zu 2
cresc. poco a poco
Cor.
(A)
Tr.
(D)
Timp.
ff

Fl.
Ob.
Cl.
Fg.
Cor.
(A)
Tr.
(D)
Timp.
Vl.
Vla.
Vc.
Cb.
1.
pp
cresc.

370
Fl.
Ob.
Cl.
Fg.
Cor.
(A)
Tr.
(D)
Timp.
Vl.
Vla.
Vc.
Cb.
ff
1.
p cresc.
pp
cresc.
ff Bassi

Fl.
ff
sf
Ob.
Cl.
Fg.
Cor
(A)
zu 2
Tr.
(D)
Timp.
Vl.
Vla.
Vc.
Cb.

380
Fl.
Ob.
Cl.
Fg.
zu 2
Cor (A)
Tr. (D)
Pk.
ten.
Vl.
Vla.
ten.
Vc. Cb.

390
Fl.
Ob.
Cl.
Fg.
Cor. (A)
Tr. (D)
Timp.
Vl.
Vla.
Vc. Cb.
p
pp
sempre pp

400
Fl.
Ob.
Cl.
Fg.
Cor. (A)
Vl.
Vla.
Vc.
Cb.
sempre pp
pp
1.
2.

410
Fl.
cresc.
Cl.
cresc.
Fg.
cresc.
Cor. (A)
p
cresc.
cresc.
Tr. (D)
1.
p
poco cresc.
Timp.
p
poco cresc.
Vl.
cresc.
cresc.
Vla.
cresc.
Vc.
cresc.
Cb.
cresc.

420
Fl.
Ob.
Cl.
Fg.
Cor. (A)
Tr. (D)
Timp.
Vl.
Vla.
Vc.
Cb.
più cresc.

Fl.
Ob.
Cl.
Fg.
Cor. (A)
Tr. (D)
zu 2
Timp.
Vl.
Vla.
Vc.
Cb.
ff

480
Fl.
Ob.
Cl.
Fg.
Cor. (A)
Tr. (D)
Timp.
Vl.
Vla.
Vc.
Cb.

Fl.
Ob.
Cl.
Fg.
zu 2
Cor.
(A)
Tr.
(D)
Timp.
Vl.
Vla.
Vc.
Cb.

440
zu 2
Fl.
zu 2
Ob.
Cl.
Fg.
Cor. (A)
zu 2
Tr. (D)
Timp.
Vl.
Vla.
Vc.
Cb.

450
Fl.
ff
Ob.
ff
Cl.
ff
Fg.
ff
Cor. (A)
ff
Tr. (D)
Timp.
Vl.
Vla.
Vc. Cb.
Bassi

II

Allegretto (♩= 76)
10
2 Flauti
2 Oboi
2 Clarinetti in A
2 Fagotti
2 Corni in E
2 Trombe in D
Timpani in A-E
Violino I
Violino II
Viola
Violoncello I
Violoncello II e Contrabasso
f
pp
ten.
p
20
Vla.
Vc.
Cb.
30
Vl. 2

Vl.2
Vla
Vc.
Cb.
40
Vl.2
Vla.
Vc.
Cb.
pp
pp
pp
pp
50
ten.
Vl.
p cresc.
poco
a
poco
cresc.
Vla
Vc.
Cb.
60
Vl.
Vla.
Vc.
Cb.

Ob.
Fg.
cresc.
cresc.
Vl.
f
f
più f
più f
Vla.
f
più f
Vc.
f
più f
Cb.
f
più f
70
Fl.
cresc.
ten.
ff
zu 2 ten.
ff
Cl. (A)
ten.
ff
Fg.
ten.
ff
Cor. (E)
cresc.
ten.
ff
Tr. (D)
ff
Timp.
ff
Vl.
ff
ff
Vla.
3
Vc.
3
3
ff
Cb.
3
3
ff

80
Fl.
Ob.
zu 2
ten.
Cl.
(A)
Fg.
Cor.
(E)
Tr.
(D)
Timp.
Vl.
Vla.
Vc.
Cb.

90
Fl.
Ob.
zu 2
Cl.
(A)
zu 2
Fg.
Cor.
(E)
Tr.
(D)
Timp.
Vl.
3
Vla.
Vc.
Cb.

Fl.
Ob.
Cl. (A)
Fg.
Cor. (E)
Tr. (D)
Timp.
Vl.
Vla.
Vc.
Cb.
dimin.
sempre dimin.
zu 2
1.
p
ten.
100
dolce
pizz.

110
Fl.
Ob.
Cl. (A)
Fg.
Tr. (D)
Vl.
Vla.
Vc. Cb.
p
p
p
Fl.
Ob.
Cl. (A)
Fg.
Cor. (E)
Tr. (D)
Vl.
Vla.
Vc. Cb.
1.
2.
p

120
Ob.
1.
Cl. (A)
Fg.
zu 2
Cor (E)
Vl.
Vla.
Vc. Cb.
cresc.
130
dimin.
p

Fl. Ob. Cl. (A) Fg. Cor. (E) Vl. Vla. Vc. Cb.

1. dolce dimin. p

1 dimin. p

dimin. p

1. dimin. p

dimin. p

dimin. p

dimin. p

dimin. p

140

Fl. Ob. Fg. Cor. (E) Tr. (D) Timp. Vl. Vla. Vc. Cb.

cresc. f sf

cresc. f sf

1. cresc. f sf

zu 2 pp 1. cresc.

pp pp

pp pp

cresc. sf

cresc. sf f

cresc.

cresc.

150
Fl.
Ob.
Cl. (A)
Fg.
Cor. (E)
Tr. (D)
Timp.
Vl.
Vla.
Vc. Cb.
ff zu 2
p dolce
ff
pizz.
p
arco
f
Fl.
Ob.
Fg.
Vl.
sempre stacc.
Vla.
Vc. Cb.

160
Fl.
Ob.
Fg.
Vl.
Vla
Vc.
Cb.
sempre p
sempre p
Fl.
Ob.
Fg.
Vl.
Vla.
Vc.
Cb.

170
Fl.
Ob.
Fg.
Tr. (D)
Timp.
Vl.
Vla.
Vc. Cb.
180
cresc.
dimin.

1. 1.

Fl. Ob. Fg. Tr. (D) Timp.

pp pp

Vl. arco pp pp Vla. Vc. Cb.

190

Vl. sempre pp sempre pp Vla. pp arco Vc. Cb. pp

Vl. sempre pp Vla. sempre pp Vc. Cb. sempre pp

200
Vl.
Vla.
Vc.
Cb.
Thickening of texture: to start a great cresc.
210
Fl.
Ob.
Cl.
(A)
Fg.
1.
ten.
p cresc.
zu 2
ten.
pp
cresc.
zu 2
ten.
p cresc.
zu 2
ten.
pp
cresc.
cresc.
cresc.
cresc.
cresc.

Fl.
zu 2
ff
Ob.
ff
Cl.
(A)
ff
Fg.
ff
Cor
(E)
cresc.
zu 2
ff
Tr.
(D)
zu 2
cresc.
ff
Timp.
cresc.
ff
Vl.
ten.
ff
ten.
ff
Vla.
ten.
ff
Vc.
Cb.
ten.
ff

220
Fl.
Ob.
Cl (A)
Fg.
Cor. (E)
Tr. (D)
Timp.
Vl.
Vla.
Vc. Cb.
ten.
p
pizz.
dolce
1.
3

230

Fl.
p
Ob.
p
Cl. (A)
Fg.
Tr. (D)
p
Vl.
Vla.
Vc. Cb.

240

Fl.
dimin.
ten.
pp
Cl.
dimin.
zu 2 ten.
pp
Fg.
dimin.
ten.
pp
Tr. (D)
Vl.
dimin.
pp
dimin.
pp
Vla.
dimin.
pp
Vc. Cb.
dimin.
arco
pp

1.
ten.
250
ten.
Fl.
Ob.
zu 2
Cl.
(A)
Fg.
zu 2
Cor.
(E)
Tr.
(D)
Timp.
Vl.
Vla.
Vc.
Cb.
pizz.
260

261
Fl.
Ob.
Cl. (A)
Fg.
Cor. (E)
Vl.
Vla.
Vc. Cb.
pp
zu 2
270
ten.
arco
f

III

Presto (𝅗𝅥. = 132)

2 Flauti

2 Oboi

2 Clarinetti in A

2 Fagotti

2 Corni in D (zu 2)

2 Trombe in D (zu 2)

Timpani in F-A

Violino I

Violino II

Viola

Violoncello e Contrabasso

f *p*

10

Fl. — 1. *cresc.* *sf*

Fg.

Vl. — *cresc.* *sf*

Vla. — *cresc.* *sf*

Vc. — *cresc.* *sf*

Cb. — *cresc.* *sf*

zu 2
20
Fl.
Ob.
Cl (A)
Fg.
Cor. (D)
Tr. (D)
Timp.
Vl.
Vla.
Vc. Cb.
Bassi
30
Fl.
Cl. (A)
Timp.
Vl.
Vla.
Vc. Cb.

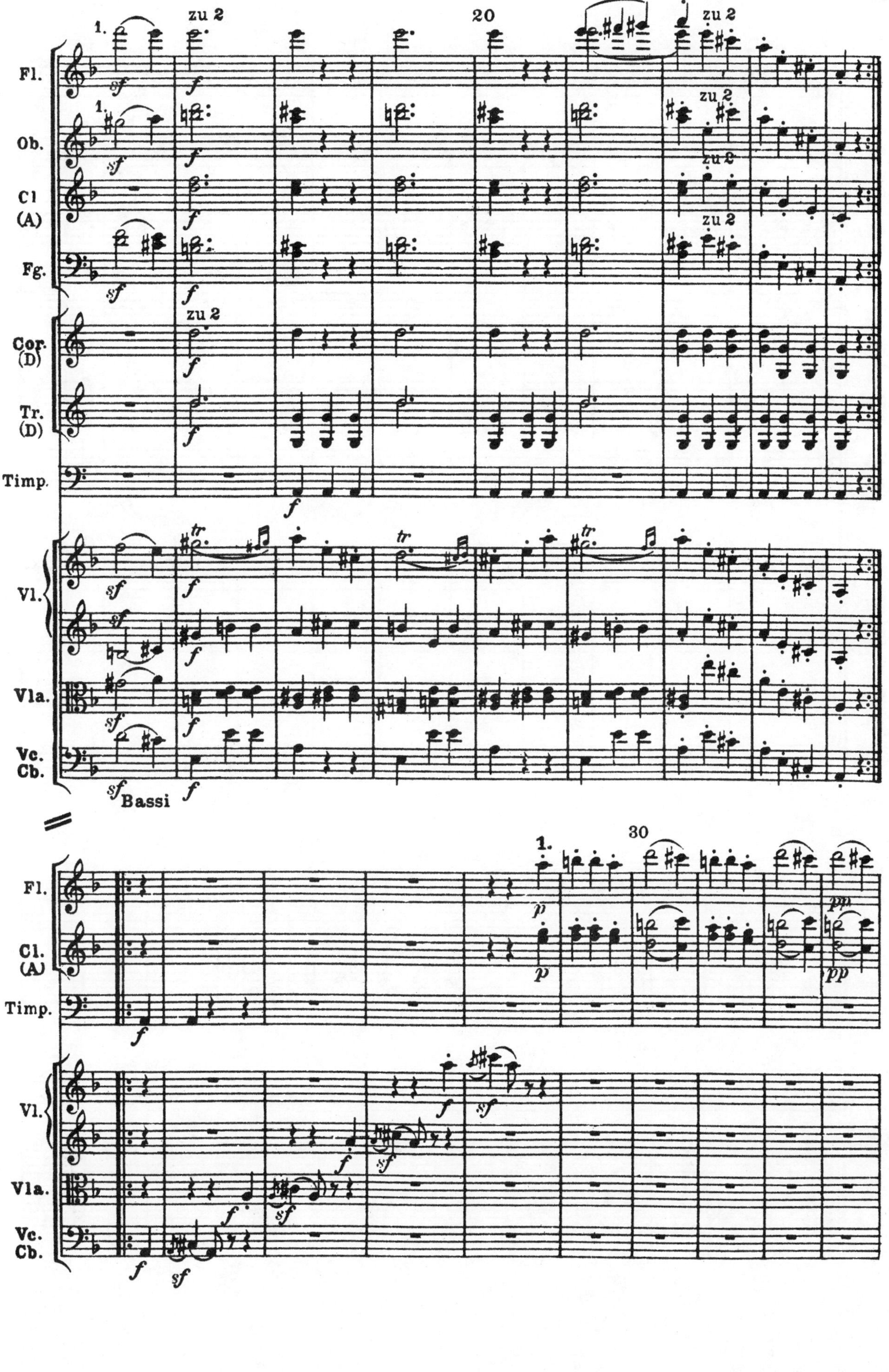

1.
40
Fl.
Ob.
Cl.
(A)
Fg.
Cor.
(D)
Tr.
(D)
Vl.
Vla.
Vc.
Cb.
50
Fl.
Ob.
Vl.
Vla

60
1.
Ob.
p dolce
Fg.
pp
ff
p dolce
zu 2
Cor.
(D)
ff
zu 2
Tr.
(D)
ff
Timp.
Vl.
ff
p
Vla.
pp
pizz.
Vc.
Cb.
70
Fl.
p cresc. poco a
cresc. poco a
cresc. poco a
arco
cresc. poco a
cresc. poco a
cresc. poco a
cresc. poco a

1.
80
Fl.
poco
1.
Ob.
poco
Fg.
poco
1.
Vl.
poco
poco
cresc.
Vla.
poco
arco
Vc.
Cb.
poco
90
Fl.
f
ff
Ob.
f
ff
Cl.
(A)
f
ff
zu 2
Fg.
f
ff
zu 2
Cor.
(D)
f
ff
Tr.
(D)
f
ff
Timp.
f
ff
Vl.
cresc.
f
ff
f
ff
Vla.
f
ff
Vc.
Cb.
f
ff

100

Fl. 1. *p*

Ob. 1. *p*

Cl. (A)

Fg. 1. *p* *p*

Cor. (D) zu 2 *pp*

Tr. (D)

Timp. *pp*

Vl. *p* *p*

Vla. *p*

Vc. pizz. *p* arco

Cb. pizz.

110

Ob. *p*

Fg. *p*

Vl. *p* cresc. *f* *sf* *sf* *sf* tr

Vl. *p* cresc. *f* *sf* *sf* *sf* *p*

Vla. *p* cresc. *f* *sf* *sf* *sf* *p*

Vc. *p* cresc. *f* *sf* *sf* *sf* *p*

Cb. arco cresc. *f* *sf* *sf* *sf* *p*

120
Fl.
Ob.
Cl. (A)
Fg.
Vl.
Vla.
Vc. Cb.
Bassi
cresc.
130
Cor. (D)
Tr. (D)
Timp.
zu 2

zu 2
140
Fl.
Ob.
Cl. (A)
zu 2
Fg.
zu 2
Cor. (D)
zu2
Tr. (D)
Timp.
Vl.
Vla.
Vc. Cb.
sf

1.
2.
Assai me-
Fl.
Ob.
Cl.
(A)
Fg.
Cor.
(D)
Tr.
(D)
Pk.
Vl.
Vla.
Vc.
Cb.
zu 2
zu 2
sf
ff
p
p dolce
150
no presto. (𝅗𝅥 = 84)
Cl
(A)
Fg.
Cor.
(D)
Vl.

160
170
Fl.
Ob.
Cl. (A)
Fg.
Cor. (D)
Vl.
p
zu 2
180

1.
Fl.
p dolce
1.
Ob.
p dolce
Cl.
(A)
p dolce
Fg
p dolce
Cor.
(D)
2.
p dolce
Vl.
190
Fl.
Ob.
Cl.
(A)
Fg.
Cor
(D)
Vl.

200
Fl.
Ob.
cresc.
Cl. (A)
cresc.
Fg.
cresc.
Cor. (D)
cresc.
Vl.
cresc.
cresc.
210
Fl.
cresc.
ff
Ob.
ff
Cl. (A)
ff
Fg.
cresc.
ff
Cor. (D)
ff
Tr. (D)
ff
tr
Timp.
ff
Vl.
ff
ff
Vla
cresc.
ff
Vc. Cb.
cresc.
ff

220
Fl.
Ob
Cl.
(A)
zu 2
Fg.
zu 2
Cor.
(D)
fp
Tr.
(D)
tr
tr
Timp.
Vl.
Vla.
Vc.
Cb.
2.
230
Cor.
(D)
sempre dim.
Vl.
p
sempre dim.
p
sempre dim.
Vla.
p
sempre dim.
Vc.
Cb.
p
sempre dim.

Presto
240
Fl.
Ob.
Cl. (A)
Fg.
Cor. (D)
Tr. (D)
Timp.
Vl.
Vla.
Vc. Cb.
zu 2
zu 2
Fl.
Fg.
Vl.
Vla.
Vc.
Cb.
1.
cresc.

250
sf
sf
zu 2
f
Fl.
Ob.
Cl.
(A)
Fg.
zu 2
Cor.
(D)
Tr.
(D)
Timp
tr.
Vl.
Vla.
Vc.
Cb.
Bassi

260

Fl.
sempre p

Ob.
p

Cl. (A)
p

Fg.
p
sempre p

Cor. (D)
p

Tr. (D)
p

Timp
p

Vl.
p
sempre p

Vla.
p
sempre p

Vc. Cb.
p
sempre p

270

Fl.

Ob.
p

Fg.

Vl.

Vla.

Vc.

Cb

280
Fl.
sempre p
Ob.
sempre p
Cl.
(A)
sempre p
Fg.
sempre p
Cor.
(D)
sempre p
Tr.
(D)
sempre p
Timp.
sempre p
tr
Vl.
Vla.
Vc.
Cb.
Bassi
p
1.
290
Fl.
p
Cl.
(A)
p
Timp.
Vl.
p
Vla.
p
Vc.
Cb.

300
Fl.
Ob.
Cl. (A)
Fg.
Cor. (D)
Tr. (D)
Vl.
Vla.
Vc Cb.
1.
pp
p
310

320
Ob.
1.
p dolce
Fg.
pp
pp
1.
p dolce
Cor. (D)
pp
Tr. (D)
pp
Timp.
pp
Vl.
pp
p
pizz.
pp
p
Vla.
pp
pp
p
Vc. Cb.
pp
pp
pizz.
p
330
Fl.
1
p cresc. poco a poco
Ob.
cresc. poco a poco
Fg.
p
cresc. poco a poco
Vl.
arco
cresc. poco a poco
cresc. poco a poco
Vla.
cresc. poco a poco
Vc. Cb.
cresc. poco a poco

340
Fl.
Ob.
Fg.
Vl.
Vla.
Vc.
Cb.
arco
cresc.
350
Cl.
(A)
Cor.
(D)
Tr.
(D)
Timp.
zu 2
f
ff

1.
360
Fl.
1.
p
Ob.
p
Cl.
(A)
1.
Fg.
p
p
Cor.
(D)
pp
Tr.
(D)
Timp.
pp
Vl.
p
p
Vla.
p
pizz.
arco
Vc.
p
pizz.
Cb.
p
370
Ob.
p
Fg.
p
Vl.
p
cresc.
f
sf
sf
sf
p
cresc.
f
sf
sf
sf
Vla.
p
cresc.
f
sf
sf
sf
Vc.
p
cresc.
f
sf
sf
sf
arco
Cb.
cresc.
f
sf
sf
sf

380

Fl.

p

Ob.

p

Cl. (A)

p

Fg.

p

ff *ff* *ff* *ff*

Vl.

p *p* *cresc.* *cresc.* *ff* *ff*

Vla.

p *cresc.* *ff*

Vc. Cb.

p Bassi *cresc.* *ff*

390

Fl.

Ob.

Cl. (A)

ff

Fg.

Cor. (D)

zu 2

Tr. (D)

f

Timp.

f

Vl.

Vla.

Vc. Cb.

400
Fl.
Ob.
Cl.
(A)
Fg.
Cor.
(D)
Tr.
(D)
Timp.
Vl.
Vla.
Vc.
Cb.
sf

Assai meno presto
410
Fl.
Ob.
Cl. (A)
Fg.
Cor. (D)
Tr. (D)
Timp.
Vl.
Vla.
Vc. Cb.
sf
p
p dolce
420
Cl (A)
Fg.
Cor. (D)
Vl.

430
Fl.
Ob.
Cl. (A)
Fg.
Cor. (D)
Vl.
p
440
Fl.
Ob.
Cl. (A)
Fg.
Cor. (D)
Vl.

1.
Fl.
p dolce
1.
Ob.
p dolce
Cl. (A)
p dolce
Fg.
p dolce
2.
Cor. (D)
p dolce
Vl.
450
Fl.
Ob.
Cl. (A)
Fg.
Cor. (D)
Vl.

460
Fl.
Ob.
Cl. (A)
Fg.
Cor. (D)
Vl.
Vla.
Vc. Cb.
cresc.
470
Tr. (D)
Timp.
ff
tr

480
Fl.
Ob.
Cl.
(A)
Fg.
Cor.
(D)
fp
sempre dim.
Tr.
(D)
tr
Timp.
Vl.
p
sempre dim.
Vla.
Vc.
Cb
2.
490
pp
ppp
Vc.
Cb.

Presto
500
Fl.
Ob.
Cl.
(A)
Fg.
Cor.
(D)
Tr.
(D)
Timp.
Vl.
Vla.
Vc.
Cb.
f
p
cresc.
510
sf
Fl.
Ob.
Fg.
Vl.
Vla.
Vc.
Cb

520
Fl.
Ob.
Cl.
(A)
Fg.
Cor.
(D)
Tr.
(D)
Timp.
Vl.
Vla.
Vc.
Cb.
Bassi
530
1.
Fl.
Cl..
(A)
Vl.
Vla.

1.
540
1.
Fl.
Ob.
Cl. (A)
Fg.
Cor. (D)
Tr. (D)
Vl.
Vla
Vc. Cb.
ff
p
pp
550
Fl.
Ob.
Fg.
Vl.
Vla.
Vc. Cb

1. 560
Ob.
p dolce
1.
Fg.
ff
p dolce
Cor. (D)
ff
Tr. (D)
ff
Timp.
ff
Vl.
ff
p
pizz.
ff
p
Vla.
ff
p
pizz.
Vc. Cb.
ff
570
Fl.
p cresc. poco a poco
Ob.
cresc. poco a poco
Fg.
p
cresc. poco a poco
arco
Vl.
cresc. poco a poco
cresc. poco a poco
Vla.
cresc. poco a poco
Vc. Cb.
cresc. poco a poco

580
Fl.
1.
Ob.
Fg.
Vl.
cresc.
cresc.
Vla.
arco
Vc.
Cb.
590
Fl.
f
ff
Ob.
Cl.
(A)
Fg.
zu 2
Cor.
(D)
Tr.
(D)
Timp
Vl.
Vla.
Vc.
Cb.

600
Fl.
Ob.
Cl. (A)
Fg.
Cor. (D)
Tr. (D)
Timp
Vl.
Vla.
Vc.
Cb.
pizz.
arco
610
cresc.

620

Fl.
Ob.
Cl. (A)
Fg.
Vl.
Vla.
Vc. Cb.
p
cresc.
p Bassi
tr
Fl.
Ob.
Cl. (A)
Fg.
Cor (D)
Tr. (D)
Timp.
Vl.
Vla.
Vc. Cb.
ff
f
zu 2

630
Fl.
Ob
Cl.
(A)
Fg.
Cor.
(D)
Tr.
(D)
Timp.
Vl.
Vla.
Vc.
Cb.

640
Coda
Fl.
Ob.
Cl.
(A)
Fg.
Cor.
(D)
Tr.
(D)
Timp.
Vl.
Vla.
Vc.
Cb.

Assai meno presto
Presto 650
Fl.
Ob.
Cl.
(A)
Fg.
Cor.
(D)
Tr.
(D)
Timp.
Vl.
Vla.
Vc.
Cb.
p
p dolce
ff

IV

Allegro con brio (𝅗𝅥 = 72)

10
1.
Fl.
Ob.
Cl.
Fg.
Cor. (A)
Tr. (D)
Timp.
Vl.
Vla.
Vc. Cb.
sf

2.
Fl.
Ob.
Cl.
Fg.
Cor. (A)
Tr. (D)
Pk.
Vl.
Vla.
Vc. Cb.

1.
2.
20
Fl.
Ob.
Cl.
Fg.
Cor.
(A)
Tr.
(D)
Timp.
Vl.
Vla
Vc.
Cb.
sf

Fl.
Ob.
Cl.
Fg.
Cor. (A)
Tr. (D)
zu 2
Timp.
Vl.
Vla.
Vc. Cb.
ff

zu 2
80
Fl.
ff
Ob.
Cl.
Fg.
Cor. (A)
zu 2
Tr. (D)
Timp.
Vl.
Vla.
Vc. Cb.

Fl.
Ob.
Cl.
Fg.
Cor. (A)
Tr. (D)
Timp.
Vl.
Vla.
Vc. Cb.

40
Fl.
Ob.
Fg.
Cor.
(A)
Tr.
(D)
Timp
Vl.
Vla.
Vc.
Cb.
50
Fl.
Ob.
Cl.
Fg.
Vl.
Vla.
Vc.
Cb.

zu 2
Fl.
Ob.
Cl.
Fg
Cor.
(A)
Tr.
(D)
Timp.
Vl.
Vla.
Vc.
Cb.

60

Fl.
Ob.
Cl.
Fg.
Cor (A)
Tr. (D)
Timp.
Vl.
Vla.
Vc. Cb.

f p 1. pizz. arco

70

Fl.
Fg.
Vl.
Vla.
Vc. Cb.

p 1. dim. pizz.

Fl.
Ob.
Cl.
Fg.
Cor. (A)
Tr. (D)
Timp.
Vl.
Vla.
Vc.
Cb.
ten.
1.
p dolce
80
arco

Fl.
Ob.
Cl.
Fg.
Cor. (A)
Tr. (D)
Timp.
Vl.
Vla.
Vc.
Cb.
ten.
1.

90
Fl.
cresc. poco a poco
Ob.
cresc. poco a poco
Cl.
cresc. poco a poco
Fg.
cresc. poco a poco
Tr.
(D)
Timp.
p cresc. poco a poco
Vl.
cresc. poco a poco
cresc. poco a poco
Vla.
cresc. poco a poco
Vc.
cresc. poco a poco
Cb.
cresc.
100
Fl.
Ob.
Cl.
Fg.
Timp.
Vl.
Vla.
Vc.
Cb.

110
Fl.
Ob.
Cl.
Fg.
zu 2
Cor. (A)
Tr. (D)
Timp.
Vl.
Vla.
Vc.
Cb.

Fl.
Ob.
Cl.
Fg.
Cor.
(A)
zu 2
Tr.
(D)
Timp.
Vl.
Vla.
Vc.
Cb.

120
1.
2.
zu 2
Fl.
Ob.
Cl.
Fg.
Cor. (A)
Tr. (D)
Timp.
Vl.
Vla.
Vc.
Cb.
sf
ff
(𝄋 Pag. 272)

Fl.
Ob.
Cl.
Fg.
Cor. (A)
Tr. (D)
Timp.
Vl.
Vla.
Vc.
Cb.
sf

130
Fl.
Ob.
Cl.
Fg.
Cor.
(A)
Tr.
(D)
Timp.
Vl.
Vla.
Vc.
Cb.
140
Vl.
Vla.
Kb.
Vc.
Cb.
Vc.

150
Fl.
Ob
Cl.
Fg.
zu 2
Cor (A)
Tr. (D)
Timp.
Vl.
Vla.
Vc. Cb.
Bassi

1.
2.
Fl.
Ob.
Cl.
Fg.
Cor.
(A)
Tr.
(D)
Timp
Vl.
Vla.
Vc.
Cb.
sf

Fl.
Ob.
Cl.
Fg.
Cor. (A)
zu 2
Tr. (D)
Timp.
Vl.
Vla.
Vc. Cb.

160
1.
2.
Fl.
Ob.
Cl.
Fg.
Cor.
(A)
Tr.
(D)
Timp.
Vl.
Vla.
Vc.
Cb.
sf

Fl.
Ob.
Cl.
Fg.
Tr. (D)
Timp.
Vl.
Vla.
Vc. Cb.

zu 2 *sf*

170

Fl.
Ob.
Cl.
Fg.
Tr. (D)
Timp.
Vl.
Vla.
Vc. Cb.

zu 2 *sf*

zu 2
180
Fl.
Ob.
Cl.
Fg.
Tr.
(D)
Vl.
Vla.
Vc.
Cb.
190
Fl.
Ob.
zu 2
Cl.
Fg.
Cor.
(A)
zu 2
Tr.
(D)
Timp.
Vl.
Vla.
Vc.
Cb.

Fl.
Ob.
Cl.
Fg.
Cor. (A)
Tr. (D)
Timp.
Vl.
Vla.
Vc. Cb.
zu 2
dimin.
200
pp

210

Fl.
Ob.
Cl.
Fg.
Timp.
Vl.
Vla.
Vc.
Cb.

pp pp pp pp pp pp pp pp pp pp

Fl.
Ob.
Cl.
Fg.
Timp.
Vl.
Vla.
Vc.
Cb.

Bassi

cresc. cresc. cresc. cresc. cresc.

x20
Fl.
Ob.
Cl.
Fg.
Cor. (A)
zu 2
Tr. (D)
Timp.
Vl.
Vla.
Vc.
Kb.
ff
sf
cresc.

230
1.
Fl.
Ob.
Cl.
Fg.
Cor. (A)
Tr. (D)
Timp.
Vl.
Vla.
Vc. Cb.
Bassi
sf

2.
zu 2
Fl.
Ob.
Cl.
Fg.
Cor. (A)
zu 2
Tr. (D)
Timp.
Vl.
Vla.
Vc. Cb.
ff

240
zu 2
Fl.
Ob.
Cl.
Fg.
Cor. (A)
zu 2
Tr. (D)
Timp.
Vl.
Vla.
Vc. Cb.
ff

250
Fl.
Ob.
Cl.
Fg.
Cor. (A)
Tr. (D)
Timp.
Vl.
Vla.
Vc. Cb.

Fl.
Ob.
Cl.
Fg.
Cor. (A)
Tr. (D)
Timp.
Vl.
Vla.
Vc. Cb.

260
Fl.
Ob.
Cl.
Fg.
Cor.
(A)
Tr.
(D)
Timp.
Vl.
Vla.
Vc.
Cb.

270
Fl.
Ob.
Cl.
Fg.
Cor. (A)
Tr. (D)
Timp.
Vl.
Vla.
Vc. Cb.

zu 2
Fl.
Ob.
Cl.
Fg.
2.
Cor.
(A)
Tr.
(D)
Timp.
Vl.
Vla.
pizz.
Vc.
Cb.

280
Fl.
Cor. (A)
2.
Vl.
dimin.
Vla.
Vc. Cb.
1.
Ob.
Cl.
Fg.
Tr. (D)
Timp.
ten.
arco
Vc.
Cb.

290
1.
Fl.
p dolce
Cl.
p dolce
Fg.
p dolce
Cor. (A)
p dolce
Vl.
Vla.
Vc.
300
ten.
Ob.
Tr. (D)
Timp.
Cb.

Fl.
Cl.
Fg.
Cor. (A)
Timp.
Vl.
Vla.
Vc.
p dolce
p dolce
p dolce
p dolce
cresc.
cresc.
cresc.
cresc.
cresc.
p
cresc. poco
310
poco a poco
poco a poco
poco a poco
poco a poco
poco a poco
a poco
cresc. poco a poco
cresc. poco a poco
cresc. poco a poco
Cb.
cresc.

Fl.
Ob.
Cl.
Fg.
Cor. (A)
Tr. (D)
Timp.
Vl.
Vla.
Vc.
Cb.
zu 2
ff

320
Fl.
Ob.
Cl.
Fg.
Cor. (A)
Tr. (D)
Timp.
Vl.
Vla.
Vc.
Cb.

330
Fl.
Ob.
Cl.
Fg.
Cor. (A)
zu 2
Tr. (D)
zu 2
Timp.
Vl.
Vla.
Vc.
Cb.

Fl.
Ob.
Cl.
Fg.
Cor. (A)
Tr. (D)
Timp.
Vl.
Vla.
Vc.
Cb.
sf

340
Fl.
Ob.
Cl.
Fg.
Cor (A)
Tr. (D)
Timp.
Vl.
Vla.
Vc.
Cb.

350

Fl.
Ob.
Cl.
Fg.
Cor. (A)
Tr. (D)
Timp.
Vl.
Vla.
Vc. Cb.

Bassi

Fl.
Ob.
Cl.
Fg.
Tr. (D)
Vl.
Vla.
Vc. Cb.

zu 2
360
Hb.
Kl.
Cor.
(A)
Tr.
(D)
Pk.
Vl.
Vla.
Vc.
Cb.
zu 2
Fl.
Ob.
zu 2
Cl.
Fg.
Cor.
(A)
Tr.
(D)
Timp.
Vl.
Vla.
Vc.
Cb.

370
Fl.
Ob.
Cl.
Fg.
Tr. (D)
f
Vl.
Vla.
Vc. Cb.
380
Timp.

Fl.
Ob.
Cl.
Fg.
Cor. (A)
Tr. (D)
Timp
Vl.
Vla.
Vc. Cb.
Kb.
Vc.
f

400
Fl.
Ob.
Cl.
Fg.
Cor. (A)
Tr. (D)
Timp.
Vl.
Vla.
Vc. Cb.
f
sempre più
ff

410
zu 2
zu 2
zu 2
Fl.
Ob.
Cl.
Fg.
Cor. (A)
Tr. (D)
Timp.
Vl.
Vla.
Vc. Cb.
sf
sf
sf
sf
sf

zu 2
420
Fl.
Ob.
Cl.
Fg.
Cor. (A)
Tr. (D)
zu 2
Timp.
Vl.
sf
sf
Vla
sf
Vc. Cb.
Bassi

zu 2
Fl.
Ob.
Cl.
Fg.
Cor.
(A)
Tr.
(D)
Timp.
Vl.
Vla.
Vc.
Cb.
fff

430
zu 2
Fl.
sf
sf
sf
sf
p
cresc. -
Ob.
cresc. -
zu 2
Cl.
Fg.
Cor. (A)
Tr. (D)
zu 2
Timp.
Vl.
Vla.
Vc.
Cb.

440
Fl.
Ob.
zu 2
Cl.
Fg.
zu 2
Cor. (A)
Tr. (D)
Timp.
Vl.
p cresc.
p cresc.
Vla.
Vc.
Cb.
fff

450
zu 2
Fl.
Ob.
Cl.
Fg.
Cor. (A)
zu 2
Tr. (D)
Timp.
Vl.
Vla.
Vc.
Cb.

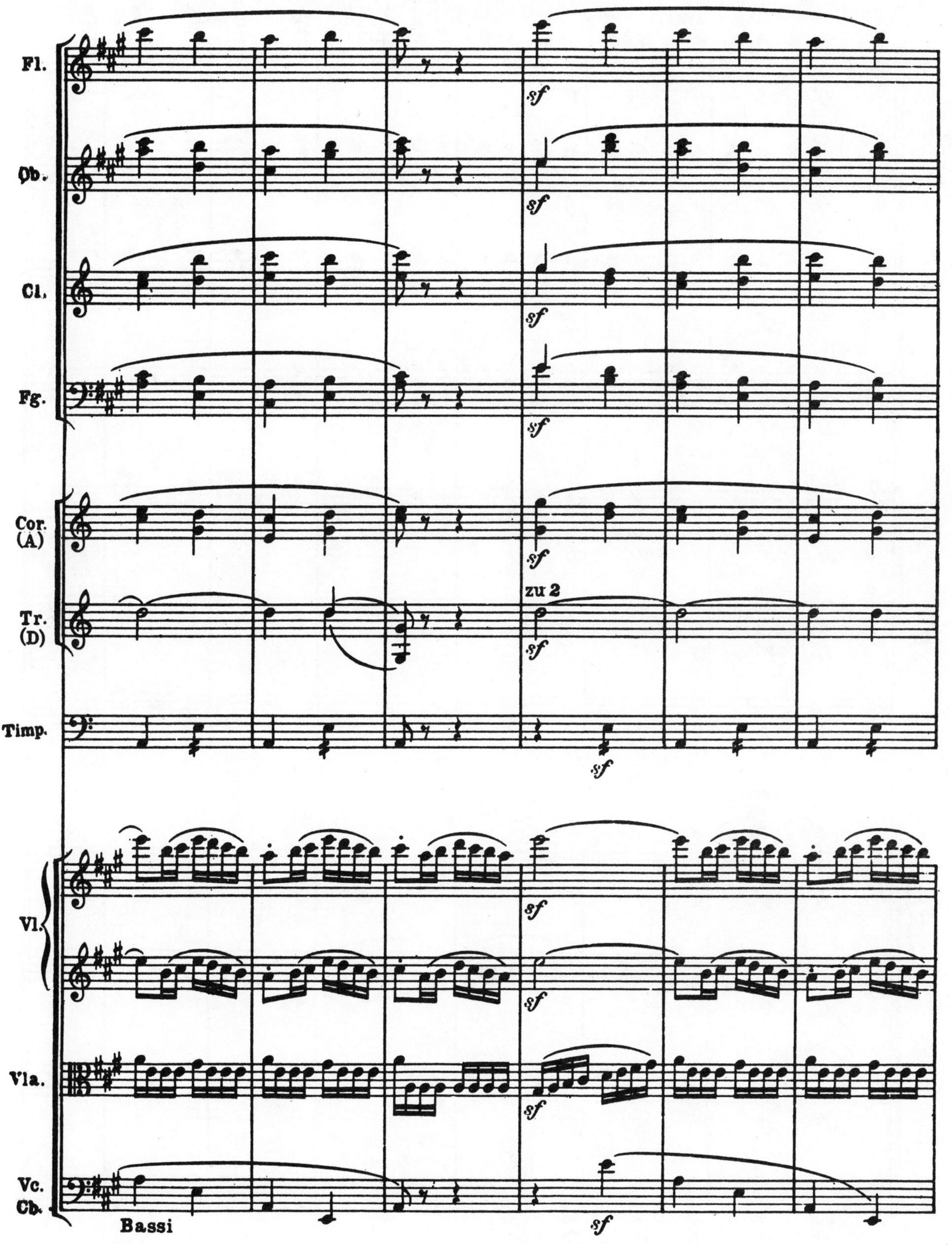
Fl.
Ob.
Cl.
Fg.
Cor. (A)
Tr. (D)
zu 2
Timp.
Vl.
Vla.
Vc.
Cb.
Bassi
sf

460
Fl.
Ob.
Cl.
Fg.
Cor. (A)
Tr. (D)
Timp.
Vl.
Vla.
Vc. Cb.
ff
sf
6